TREY ALLEN
A. FLEMING BELL, II

Suggested
Procedural
Rules for Local
Appointed Boards

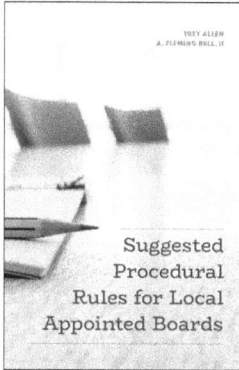

Access an Electronic Version of the Procedural Rules

Purchase of this book includes a FREE electronic version of the procedural rules that can be customized to fit a particular board's specific needs.

Access and download the rules in RTF format at **sog.unc.edu/pubs/9781560119876**.

For information about other publications and resources from the School of Government, visit **sog.unc.edu**.

TREY ALLEN
A. FLEMING BELL, II

Suggested Procedural Rules for Local Appointed Boards

The School of Government at the University of North Carolina at Chapel Hill works to improve the lives of North Carolinians by engaging in practical scholarship that helps public officials and citizens understand and improve state and local government. Established in 1931 as the Institute of Government, the School provides educational, advisory, and research services for state and local governments. The School of Government is also home to a nationally ranked Master of Public Administration program, the North Carolina Judicial College, and specialized centers focused on community and economic development, information technology, and environmental finance.

As the largest university-based local government training, advisory, and research organization in the United States, the School of Government offers up to 200 courses, webinars, and specialized conferences for more than 12,000 public officials each year. In addition, faculty members annually publish approximately 50 books, manuals, reports, articles, bulletins, and other print and online content related to state and local government. The School also produces the *Daily Bulletin Online* each day the General Assembly is in session, reporting on activities for members of the legislature and others who need to follow the course of legislation.

Operating support for the School of Government's programs and activities comes from many sources, including state appropriations, local government membership dues, private contributions, publication sales, course fees, and service contracts.

Visit sog.unc.edu or call 919.966.5381 for more information on the School's courses, publications, programs, and services.

Michael R. Smith, DEAN
Thomas H. Thornburg, SENIOR ASSOCIATE DEAN
Jen Willis, ASSOCIATE DEAN FOR DEVELOPMENT
Michael Vollmer, ASSOCIATE DEAN FOR ADMINISTRATION

FACULTY

Whitney Afonso
Trey Allen
Gregory S. Allison
Lydian Altman
David N. Ammons
Ann M. Anderson
Maureen Berner
Frayda S. Bluestein
Kirk Boone
Mark F. Botts
Anita R. Brown-Graham
Peg Carlson
Connor Crews
Leisha DeHart-Davis
Shea Riggsbee Denning
Sara DePasquale

Jacquelyn Greene
Margaret F. Henderson
Norma Houston
Cheryl Daniels Howell
Willow S. Jacobson
Robert P. Joyce
Diane M. Juffras
Dona G. Lewandowski
Adam Lovelady
James M. Markham
Christopher B. McLaughlin
Kara A. Millonzi
Jill D. Moore
Jonathan Q. Morgan
Ricardo S. Morse
C. Tyler Mulligan

Kimberly L. Nelson
David W. Owens
William C. Rivenbark
Dale J. Roenigk
John Rubin
Jessica Smith
Meredith Smith
Carl W. Stenberg III
John B. Stephens
Charles Szypszak
Shannon H. Tufts
Aimee N. Wall
Jeffrey B. Welty (on leave)
Richard B. Whisnant

Printed in the United States of America

29 28 27 26 25   2 3 4 5 6

5ISBN 978-1-56011-987-6

Contents

Preface

This handbook replaces *Suggested Rules of Procedure for Small Local Government Boards*, a popular publication first authored by Bonnie E. Davis and revised and expanded by A. Fleming Bell, II. The widespread use of that publication shows that it succeeded in providing local government boards with a concise set of model rules that they found helpful to their work.

This handbook incorporates material from *Suggested Rules of Procedure for Small Local Government Boards*, though the two publications differ in significant ways. Intervening changes in the law have been taken into account. Many of the rules and the accompanying explanatory comments have been substantially rewritten. New rules have been added, and some rules have been eliminated, combined with other rules, or divided into separate rules. The goal throughout has been to make the rules easier to understand and apply whenever possible.

Extensive footnotes also distinguish this handbook from *Suggested Rules of Procedure for Small Local Government Boards*. City councils and boards of county commissioners enjoy broad discretion to decide the structure and functions of most local appointed boards; however, some of those appointed boards are subject to their own statutory procedural requirements. The footnotes attempt to document those requirements, particularly when they could make it necessary for a board to modify one or more of the model rules.

This handbook focuses exclusively on local *appointed* boards. An array of statutory procedural requirements peculiar to city councils or boards of county commissioners do not apply to local appointed boards. For this reason, the School of Government has published a separate volume of model procedural rules for city councils and another for boards of county commissioners.

This handbook does not include procedures for quasi-judicial hearings. Local appointed boards with responsibility for those proceedings can find legal and practical guidance in *Quasi-Judicial Handbook: A Guide for Boards Making Development Regulation Decisions* (2017) by Adam Lovelady and David W. Owens.

Thanks are due to our colleagues Frayda S. Bluestein, who reviewed the manuscript and provided many valuable suggestions, and Rebecca Badgett, who helped identify pertinent statutes and checked citations. We are likewise grateful to Melissa Twomey for her fine edits and to the other professionals who assisted in bringing this handbook to publication.

Trey Allen
Associate Professor of Public Law and Government

A. Fleming Bell, II
Professor of Public Law and Government, *Emeritus*

Summer 2020

Introduction

Appointed boards are a major feature of local government in North Carolina. Cities and counties around the state rely on them to address issues involving everything from public parks to fire service. Although statutes control the appointment and duties of some local appointed boards, most of these boards exist and function solely at the discretion of local governing boards (city councils or boards of county commissioners), which enjoy broad authority to "create, change, abolish, and consolidate" appointed boards "to promote [the] orderly and efficient administration" of local government affairs.[1] Most appointed boards perform purely advisory functions, but some exercise significant decision-making powers. Local boards of health, for example, perform public health policymaking, rulemaking, and adjudicatory functions, while boards of equalization and review decide certain property tax appeals.[2]

---

1. Chapter 153A, Section 76 of the North Carolina General Statutes (hereinafter G.S.) (counties); G.S. 160A-146 (cities). *See also id.* § 153A-77(a) ("The board of county commissioners may also appoint advisory boards, committees, councils and agencies composed of qualified and interested county residents to study, interpret and develop community support and cooperation in activities conducted by or under the authority of the board of county commissioners[.]").

The law limits the power of the city council or board of county commissioners to change, abolish, or consolidate certain appointed boards. *E.g.*, G.S. 130A-35(b) (specifying size and makeup of county board of health); 160D-301(a) (mandating that each city or county planning board have at least three members).

2. Jill D. Moore, *Public Health, in* County and Municipal Government in North Carolina 648 (Frayda S. Bluestein ed., 2d ed. 2014); Christopher B. McLaughlin, *Property Tax Policy and Administration, in* Introduction to Local Government Finance 117 (Kara A. Millonzi ed., 4th ed. 2018).

The model rules in this volume are intended to help local appointed boards reach informed decisions in an effective, efficient, orderly, courteous, and fair manner, regardless of the matter under consideration.[3] The content of these rules reflects the influence of parliamentary law, statutory procedural requirements, *Robert's Rules of Order Newly Revised* and similar manuals, as well as the advising that faculty members at the School of Government have done on procedural issues over the years.

Parliamentary law encompasses the "recognized rules, precedents[,] and usages of legislative bodies by which their procedure is regulated. It is that system of rules and precedents that originated in the British Parliament and . . . has been developed by legislative or deliberative bodies in this and other countries."[4] Parliamentary law has yielded a number of fundamental principles for the conduct of business by deliberative bodies.[5] With local appointed boards in mind, some of the principles may be stated as follows:

- *The board must take only those actions that lie within its authority.* Except where their powers are defined by state law, local appointed boards have only those powers granted them by their local governing boards.
- *The board must meet in order to act.* The powers granted to a local appointed board belong to the board as a whole, not to individual members, who may not act for the board except pursuant to valid delegations of authority.
- *Board members are equal participants.* Each member has the right to propose motions, to debate, to vote, and to exercise any other privilege of membership. At the same time, each member is bound by reciprocal obligations, such as the duty to protect the rights of fellow members.

---

3. *See* AMERICAN INSTITUTE OF PARLIAMENTARIANS STANDARD CODE OF PARLIAMENTARY PROCEDURE 2 (2012) (hereinafter STANDARD CODE) ("The purpose of meeting procedures is to allow members to reach informed business decisions in an effective, efficient, orderly, courteous, and fair manner.").

4. AMERICAN SOCIETY OF LEGISLATIVE CLERKS AND SECRETARIES' MASON'S MANUAL REVISION COMMISSION, MASON'S MANUAL OF LEGISLATIVE PROCEDURE § 35, p. 29 (2010 ed.) (hereinafter MASON'S MANUAL).

5. The fundamental principles listed in this introduction are taken primarily from pages 1–4 of MASON'S MANUAL and pages 6–10 of STANDARD CODE.

- *Members must receive proper notice of board meetings.* Because each member has the right to participate in meetings, members should have reasonable notice of each meeting's time, place, and purpose.
- *A quorum is necessary for the board to act.* The term "quorum" refers to the number of members who must be present for a deliberative body to take action. For some appointed boards, state law specifies the method of quorum calculation.[6] In the absence of a statutory provision on point, the default rule is that a quorum consists of more than half of a board's members.[7]
- *There must be an opportunity for debate.* The board is a deliberative body, that is, a group of persons who meet "to discuss and determine upon common action."[8] Members cannot be expected to form collective judgments unless they can exchange information and opinions concerning issues before the board.
- *Questions must be decided by voting.* Voting is the mechanism by which the board expresses its collective will.[9]
- *A majority vote is required to take action.* Inasmuch as the board operates democratically, the will of the majority is regarded as the will of the board.[10] The term "majority vote" usually means more than half of lawful votes cast, a quorum being present; however, state law or the board's own procedures may demand larger majorities for certain actions.[11]

---

6. *E.g.,* G.S. 130A-35(f) ("A majority of the members shall constitute a quorum" of a county board of health).

7. *See* Edwards v. Bd. of Educ. of Yancey Cnty., 235 N.C. 345, 348 (1952) ("The statute creating the county board of education does not specify in terms the number of members competent to transact its corporate business in the absence of other members. As a consequence, the common law rule that a majority of the whole membership is necessary to constitute a quorum applies.").

8. *Robert's Rules of Order Newly Revised* xxix (11th ed.) (hereinafter *RONR*).

9. *See* STANDARD CODE, p. 147 ("[A] vote is a formal expression of the will of the assembly.").

10. *Id.* at 135 ("[I]n an organization, the ultimate authority lies in a majority of the members when they meet to take action through majority votes. This fundamental principle of voting allows members to democratically and legitimately operate their organization.")

11. *E.g.,* G.S. 160D-406(i) ("The concurring vote of four-fifths of the board [of adjustment] shall be necessary to grant a variance.").

- *Meetings of the board must be characterized by fairness and good faith.* Part of conducting a meeting fairly is applying the board's procedural rules consistently. The consistent application of the rules ensures that members are treated the same, whatever their viewpoints on particular issues. Members who try to manipulate the board through fraud, trickery, or deception violate their obligation to act in good faith.

The above principles permeate these rules. For example, consistent with the right of members to engage in debate, Rule 25 (Motion 8) does not permit the board to entertain a motion to end debate on a pending matter until every member has had a chance to speak at least once. The requirement in Rule 27 that motions pass by majority vote recognizes the fundamental place of majority rule in deliberative bodies.

A number of these rules restate procedural requirements imposed on all local appointed boards by state law. As public bodies, the boards must abide by the public access, notice, and other provisions of the open meetings law.[12] The demands of the open meetings law are reflected most conspicuously in Part III (Open Meetings) and Part V (Types of Meetings) of this handbook. The other points at which these rules incorporate statutory requirements are too numerous to mention here but are documented in the commentary and footnotes.

Many of the specifics in these rules are not dictated by fundamental parliamentary principles or by statute. Instead, they correspond more or less to procedures recommended by *Robert's* or other prominent manuals of procedure. Local governments have broad discretion to modify or omit any provision that does not embody parliamentary or state law, even if the variation departs from *Robert's*. For instance, the restrictions in Rule 25 on motions to reconsider—who may make them and when they may be offered—could be relaxed without violating parliamentary or state law. Similarly, although Rule 21 eliminates the practice of requiring

---

12. G.S. 143-318.9, -318.18.

seconds to motions, the board could substitute its own rule to the contrary. Alternative wordings and optional language for some of the rules are shown enclosed in brackets.

Appendix A lists procedural statutes that pertain to designated local appointed boards. Appendix B summarizes in chart form Rule 25's provisions on procedural motions.

Suggested Procedural Rules

Part I. Applicability
Rule 1. Applicability of Rules

These rules apply to all meetings of the [name of city/county] Board of _____. For purposes of these rules, a meeting of the board occurs whenever a majority of the board's members gather, either in person or simultaneously by electronic means, to conduct hearings, deliberate, vote, or otherwise transact public business within the board's real or apparent jurisdiction. The term "majority" as used here and elsewhere in these rules means, unless otherwise specified, a simple majority, that is, more than half.

> **Comment:** As explained in the introduction, this publication is intended primarily for local government appointed boards. It is not meant for city councils or boards of county commissioners, both of which are subject to various legal requirements and practical considerations that do not apply to other local government boards. City councils and boards of county commissioners have separate volumes in the series to which this publication belongs: *Suggested Rules of Procedure for a City Council* and *Suggested Rules of Procedure for the Board of County Commissioners*.
>
> In North Carolina, city councils and boards of county commissioners enjoy broad authority to "create, change, abolish, and consolidate" appointed boards "to promote [the] orderly and efficient administration" of city or county

affairs.[1] State law also permits them to establish certain
appointed boards by agreement for the performance of
designated functions across multiple jurisdictions.[2]

The suggested rules in this volume incorporate statutory
requirements generally applicable to local government
boards, significant judicial decisions on procedural issues,
and fundamental parliamentary principles. Some boards
will need to modify one or more of the rules to align with
statutes peculiar to them. Although many such statutes
are referenced in the *Commentary* and footnotes, this
publication is not comprehensive in that respect. Questions

---

1. G.S. 153A-76 (counties); 160A-146 (cities). *See also id.* § 153A-77(a) ("The board
of county commissioners may also appoint advisory boards, committees, councils
and agencies composed of qualified and interested county residents to study,
interpret and develop community support and cooperation in activities conducted
by or under the authority of the board of county commissioners[.]").

The law limits the power of the city council or board of county commissioners
to change, abolish, or consolidate certain appointed boards. *E.g.*, G.S. 130A-35(b)
(specifying size and makeup of county board of health); 160D-301(a) (mandating
that each city or county planning board have at least three members).

Although this book focuses on city and county appointed boards, local boards
of education also enjoy express statutory authority to establish particular kinds of
boards or committees. *E.g.*, G.S. 115C-47(18) (local paperwork control committee);
115C-55 (school advisory councils).

2. G.S. 108A-15.7 (regional social-services department); 122C-115.1 (multi-county
area authority); 130A-36 (district board of health); 130A-45.02(b) (multi-county
public health authority); 153A-421 (regional solid waste management authority);
153A-391 (regional planning commission); 158-8 (regional economic development
commission); 160A-470 (regional council of government); 160A-479 (regional sports
authority); 160A-507 (regional redevelopment commission); 160A-507.1 (joint
county-city redevelopment commission); 160D-303(c) (joint historic preservation
commission); 160D-304(b) (joint appearance commission); 162A-3 (multi-jurisdiction
water and sewer authority); 162A-33 (multi-jurisdiction water and sewer authority);
162A-66 (metropolitan sewerage district).

Cities, counties, and other local government units can also form joint agencies
through interlocal agreements. G.S. 160A-464(3). Units may enter interlocal
agreements for the exercise of "any power, function, public enterprise, right,
privilege, or immunity of local government." *Id.* § 160A-460(1).

concerning the procedural requirements specific to certain appointed boards should be referred to the relevant local government attorney.

For the most part, city councils and boards of county commissioners may adopt procedural rules for their appointed boards, though in lots of places this has not happened. State law expressly authorizes some local appointed boards to adopt their own rules of procedure.[3] Even where express authority is lacking, an appointed board enjoys inherent authority to adopt its own procedural rules, so long as its rules do not contravene constitutional limitations, relevant statutory provisions, fundamental parliamentary principles, or any requirements imposed by the city council, board of county commissioners, or other governing body with jurisdiction over the board.[4]

---

3. *E.g.*, G.S. 153A-394 (regional planning commission "may adopt bylaws for the conduct of its business"); 153A-425 (regional solid waste management authority "shall then adopt bylaws for the conduct of its business"); 158-9 (economic development commission "shall adopt such rules and regulations not inconsistent herewith as it may deem necessary for the proper discharge of its duties"); 158-21 (county industrial commission "shall draw up and ratify . . . bylaws and procedural rules and policies"); 159B-11(a) (joint municipal electric power agency may "adopt bylaws for the regulation of the affairs and the conduct of its business, and . . . prescribe rules, regulations and policies in connection with the performance of its functions and duties"); 160A-473 (regional council of government must "adopt bylaws for the conduct of its business"); 160A-479.5 (regional sports authority "shall then adopt bylaws for the conduct of its business"); 160D-308 ("In the absence of action by the governing board, each [planning board, board of adjustment, historic preservation commission, appearance commission, housing appeals board, and other advisory boards] created under this Article is authorized to adopt its own rules of procedure that are consistent with the provisions of this Chapter."); 162A-6 (water and sewer authority may "adopt bylaws for the regulation of its affairs"); 162A-34(c) (metropolitan water district board must specify terms of office of secretary and treasurer *in its bylaws*); 162A-67(d) (same for metropolitan sewerage district board).

4. American Society of Legislative Clerks and Secretaries' Mason's Manual Revision Commission, Mason's Manual of Legislative Procedure § 2.1, p. 11 (2010 ed.) (hereinafter Mason's Manual) ("Every governmental body has an inherent right to regulate its own procedure, subject to provisions of the constitution or other controlling authority.").

The effect of Rule 1 is to make these rules applicable to any gathering of board members covered by the open meetings law, which imposes public notice, access, and other requirements on the official meetings of public bodies.[5] For purposes of that law and these rules, members are deemed to hold an official meeting whenever a majority of them come together in one place or gather simultaneously by electronic means to conduct public business within the board's real or apparent jurisdiction.[6] On the other hand, purely social and other informal gatherings do not qualify as meetings of the board unless they are called or held to evade the spirit and purposes of the open meetings law.[7]

As indicated by the word "deliberate" in Rule 1, these rules extend to gatherings at which a majority of board members discuss official business, even if they do not vote on anything.

Part II. Quorum
Rule 2. Quorum

The presence of a quorum is necessary for the board to conduct business. A quorum consists of a majority of the board's actual membership [excluding vacant seats]. [A member who withdraws from a meeting of the board without being excused by majority vote of the remaining members present shall be counted as present for quorum purposes.]

> **Comment:** The term "quorum" refers to the minimum number of members who must be present for a body to conduct business. It does not refer to the number of members who vote on a particular motion.[8]

---

5. G.S. 143-318.9–.18.

6. G.S. 143-318.10(d).

7. *Id.*

8. *Robert's Rules of Order Newly Revised* (11th ed.) (hereinafter *RONR*), p. 345, ll. 3–7 ("[A] quorum in an assembly is the number of members . . . who must be

When it comes to local government boards, the default rule in parliamentary law is that a majority of the membership is necessary to establish a quorum.[9] Statutory provisions dictate how some local government appointed boards go about determining whether a quorum is present.[10] Boards subject to such provisions should ensure that their version of Rule 2 complies with the statutory language.

By adopting the bracketed phrase in the first sentence of Rule 2, a board will exclude vacant seats from its quorum determinations. While it is acceptable for most appointed boards to choose between excluding or not excluding vacant seats, excluding them is often the best option because it can reduce the likelihood that the absence of a quorum will

---

present in order that business can be validly transacted. The quorum refers to the number of members present, not to the number actually voting in a particular question.").

9. *See* Edwards v. Bd. of Educ. of Yancey Cnty., 235 N.C. 345, 348 (1952) ("The statute creating the county board of education does not specify in terms the number of members competent to transact its corporate business in the absence of other members. As a consequence, the common law rule that a majority of the whole membership is necessary to constitute a quorum applies.").

10. G.S. 63-81(b) (quorum for special airport district board); 108A-15.8(h) (quorum for regional board of social services); 130A-35(f) (quorum for county board of health); 130A-37(g) (quorum for district board of health); 130A-45.1(i) (quorum for public health authority board); 131E-18(h) (quorum for hospital authority board); 139-41(b) (quorum for watershed improvement commission); 153A-77(c) (quorum for consolidated human services board); 157-5(d) (quorum for city or county housing authority); 157-36(k) (quorum for regional housing authority); 159B-9(e) (quorum for joint municipal electric power agency); 159B-43(e) (quorum for joint municipal assistance agency); 159C-4(d) (quorum for county industrial facilities and pollution control financing authority); 160A-510 (quorum for redevelopment commission); 160A-553 (quorum for parking authority); 160A-577 (quorum for public transportation authority); 160A-606(a) (quorum for regional public transportation authority); 160A-665 (quorum for regional natural gas district board); 162A-5(c) (quorum for water and sewer authority); 162A-34(a) (quorum for metropolitan water district board); 162A-67(d) (quorum for metropolitan sewerage district board); 162A-85.3(f) (quorum for metropolitan water and sewerage district); 163-31(d) (quorum for county board of elections).

prevent a board from performing its assigned functions.[11] Suppose that a seven-member board has two vacant seats. If the vacant seats are counted, then four members—a majority of the board's seven seats—must be present for a quorum to exist. On the other hand, if the vacant seats are excluded, then only three members—a majority of the board's five remaining members—constitute a quorum.

If adopted, the bracketed second sentence in Rule 2 denies members the power to defeat a quorum merely by stepping out of the meeting room. It tracks similar language in the quorum statutes for city councils and boards of county commissioners.[12]

Part III. Open Meetings

Rule 3. Electronic Board Meetings

(a) General Provisions. No member who is not physically present may participate in a meeting of the board by electronic means except in accordance with this rule. [Describe circumstances in

---

11. In a few cases, state law specifies the impact of vacancies on an appointed board's quorum. G.S. 63-81(b) ("No vacancy in the membership of the [special airport] district board shall impair the right of a quorum to exercise all the rights and perform all the duties of the district board."); 108A-15.8(h) (emphasis added) ("A majority of the actual membership, excluding vacancies, shall constitute a quorum" of a regional board of social services.); 159B-9(e) ("A vacancy in the board of commissioners of the joint agency shall not impair the right of a quorum to exercise all the rights and perform all the duties of the joint agency."); 159B-43(e) (same for joint municipal assistance agency); 159C-4(d) (same for county industrial facilities and pollution control financing authority); 162A-5(c) (same for [water and sewer] authority); 162A-34(a) (same for metropolitan water district board); 162A-67(d) (same for metropolitan sewerage district board); 162A-85.3(f) (same for metropolitan water and sewerage district).

12. G.S. 153A-43 ("If a member [of the board of county commissioners] has withdrawn from a meeting without being excused by majority vote of the remaining members present, he shall be counted as present for the purposes of determining whether a quorum is present."); 160A-74 (same for city council).

which members may attend meetings electronically and set out any limitations on such a member's ability to participate in the conduct of business.].

> **Comment:** The open meetings law acknowledges the possibility of remote (electronic) participation by members of public bodies.[13] Nonetheless, local government boards that wish to allow remote participation should do so pursuant to a policy that addresses key issues, such as the circumstances under which remote participation will be permitted.[14] Legal and practical considerations may lead a board to disallow remote participation during quasi-judicial hearings or closed sessions.[15] At a minimum, the policy should also address whether a member who takes part remotely (1) counts as present for quorum purposes and (2) may vote on motions before the board.

(b) Electronic Meetings During a State of Emergency Declared by the Governor or General Assembly. During any state of emergency declared by the Governor or General Assembly pursuant to G.S. 166A-19.20, a meeting of the board shall comply with the requirements of this paragraph if (1) the board falls within the emergency area and (2) at least one board member attends the meeting by conference call, conference video, or other electronic means.

(1) *Notice.* The public notice for any regular, special, emergency, or recessed meeting that is subject to this paragraph shall specify how the public can access the electronic meeting in real time.

---

13. G.S. 143-318.13(a).

14. For more on the legal and practical considerations that should inform a local government's remote participation policy, see Frayda S. Bluestein, *Remote Participation in Local Government Board Meetings*, LOC. GOV'T L. BULL. No. 133 (Aug. 2013), www.sog.unc.edu/sites/www.sog.unc.edu/files/reports/lglb133.pdf.

15. *See id.* at 7–8 (describing factors that could lead a local government not to allow remote participation during quasi-judicial hearings or closed sessions).

(2) *Member Identification.* Each member who attends by electronic means shall identify himself or herself in each of the following situations:

    a. when roll is taken or the meeting begins;

    b. before taking part in deliberations, including making any motions, proposing any amendments, or raising any points of order; and

    c. before voting.

(3) *Meeting Materials.* All documents considered during the meeting shall be furnished to each board member.

(4) *Method of Electronic Participation.* Any member who attends electronically shall use a means of communication that enables the member

    a. to hear what is said by other board members and any person who addresses the board and

    b. to be heard by other board members.

(5) *Quorum.* A member who attends by electronic means counts as present for quorum purposes, but only while the board maintains electronic communication with that member.

(6) *Voting.* The board shall conduct all votes by roll call. It may not vote by secret or written ballots. The votes of any member who attends by electronic means shall be counted as if the member were physically present, but only while the board maintains electronic communication with that member.

(6) *Acting by Reference.* The board shall not deliberate, vote, or otherwise take action on any matter by reference to the agenda or any other document unless copies of the agenda or document are available for public inspection at the meeting and so worded that persons in attendance can understand what is being deliberated or acted upon.

(7) *Minutes.* The minutes shall indicate that the meeting was conducted by electronic means, which members took part electronically, and when such members joined or left the electronic meeting.

(8) *Live Streaming.* The meeting shall be streamed live online so that live audio (and video, if any) are available to the public.

If the board meets by conference call, the public shall have an opportunity to dial in or stream the audio live and listen to the electronic meeting.

(9) *Public Hearings.* Although it may conduct any public hearing mandated or permitted by law, the board shall allow the public to submit written comments on the hearing's subject matter between the publication of any required notice and twenty-four hours after the hearing.

> **Comment:** Paragraph (b) of Rule 3 restates pertinent provisions of G.S. 166A-19.24. The statute also includes requirements for quasi-judicial hearings. These rules do not cover quasi-judicial hearings, and so they are not incorporated into paragraph (3).

Rule 4. Meetings to Be Open to the Public

Except as permitted by Rule 5, all meetings of the board shall be open to the public, and any person may attend its meetings.

> **Comment:** The presumption under the open meetings law is that a public body's meetings will be open to the public.[16] The law allows a public body to enter closed session, however, as provided in Rule 5.

Rule 5. Closed Sessions

(a) Bases for Closed Session. The board may enter a closed session from which the public is excluded on any of the grounds listed in G.S. 143-318.11(a).

> **Comment:** The open meetings law allows public bodies to hold closed sessions for any of the reasons listed in G.S. 143- 318.11(a). Rule 5 does not list the individual bases for closed sessions because most of them have no practical application to most local government appointed boards. Rarely, for example, will an appointed board need to enter closed session pursuant to G.S. 143-318.11(a)(4) to discuss matters related to the location or expansion of industries

---

16. G.S. 143-318.10(a).

or businesses in the area served by the board. The bases most likely to be used by local government appointed boards include G.S. 143- 318.11(a)(1) (prevent disclosure of privileged or confidential information or information not considered public record) and G.S. 143-318.11(a)(3) (attorney consultation and preservation of attorney-client privilege).

(b) Motion to Enter Closed Session. The board may hold a closed session only upon a motion duly made and adopted in open session. The motion to enter closed session shall cite one or more of the permissible bases listed in G.S. 143-318.11(a) for closed sessions. For a closed session held under G.S. 143-318.11(a)(1) (prevent disclosure of privileged or confidential information or information not considered public record), the motion shall name or cite the law that renders the information confidential or privileged. For a closed session called pursuant to G.S. 143-318.11(a)(3) (attorney consultation and preservation of attorney-client privilege), the motion shall name the parties to any pending lawsuit that the board's attorney plans to discuss in the closed session.

> **Comment:** Rule 5(b) restates the closed-session motion requirements found in G.S. 143-318.11(c).

(c) Closed-Session Participants. Aside from the board members themselves, only those individuals invited by the board may participate in a closed session. The board will invite only those individuals whose presence is reasonably necessary to aid the board in its closed-session deliberations.

> **Comment:** The open meetings law does not address who may attend a closed session, but it seems reasonable to assume that the board may invite non-members to attend a closed session when their presence is reasonably necessary to aid the board in its deliberations. The board's attorney must take part, either in person or by electronic means, in any closed session called pursuant to G.S. 143-318.11(a)(3) (attorney consultation and preservation of attorney-client privilege). Additionally, the board must restrict closed session attendance in some situations due to the confidential nature of the matters under

consideration. When the board meets in closed session to consult with its attorney, the board risks waiving the attorney-client privilege, and forfeiting the legal basis for the closed session, if it allows anyone to attend who is not covered by the privilege. Likewise, if the board enters closed session to examine confidential personnel records, it must exclude anyone who is not authorized to access those records.

(d) Motion to Return to Open Session. Upon completing its closed-session business, the board shall return to open session.

> **Comment:** The open meetings law does not list adjournment among the actions that a public body may take in closed session. Accordingly, the board must return to open session following the conclusion of a closed session, even if adjournment is the only remaining item of business.

Rule 6. Meeting Minutes

(a) Minutes Required for All Meetings. The board shall keep full and accurate minutes of its meetings, including any closed sessions. To be "full and accurate," the minutes must record all actions taken by the board, as well as the board's compliance with any applicable procedural requirements. The minutes should set out the precise wording of each motion and make it possible to determine the number of votes cast for and against each motion. The minutes need not record board member discussions, though the board in its discretion may decide to incorporate such details into the minutes.

> **Comment:** The open meetings law obliges public bodies to keep full and accurate minutes of their official meetings.[17]

---

17. G.S. 143-318.10(e). For an in-depth analysis of what constitutes "full and accurate" minutes, see Trey Allen, *"Full and Accurate" Minutes: A Primer,* LOC. GOV'T L. BULL. No. 140 (Jan. 2019), https://www.sog.unc.edu/sites/www.sog.unc.edu/files/reports/20180867_LGLB-140_Layout_5.pdf.

Statutes for some appointed boards also impose minutes requirements. G.S. 159B-9(d) ("The secretary or any assistant secretary of the joint [municipal electric power] agency shall keep a record of the proceedings of the joint agency[.]"); 159B-43(d) ("The secretary or any assistant secretary of the joint municipal assistance agency shall keep a record of the proceedings of the joint municipal

According to the North Carolina Supreme Court, minutes "should contain mainly a record of what was *done* at the meeting, not what was *said* by the members."[18] Why? Because the purpose of minutes "is to reflect matters such as motions made, the movant, points of order, and appeals—not to show discussion or absence of action."[19] Despite the high court's admonition, many local government boards choose to record the substance of their discussions in the minutes. Rule 6 acknowledges that reality.

The minutes should make clear the total number of votes cast for and against each motion. Some actions must be approved by more than a simple majority of votes cast, a quorum being present. If the board's adoption of a motion to take such an action were challenged on the ground that not enough members voted in favor of it, the court might examine the minutes to ascertain whether the requisite supermajority supported the motion.

Under the open meetings law, a public body's minutes "may be in written form or, at the option of the public body, may be in the form of sound or video and sound recordings."[20] Nonetheless, because the minutes of meetings of local appointed boards can qualify as essential

---

assistance agency[.]"); 159C-4(c) ("The secretary of the [county industrial facilities and pollution control financing] authority shall keep a record of the proceedings of the authority[.]"); 160D-308 (each planning board, board of adjustment, historic-preservation commission, appearance commission, housing-appeals board, or other advisory board appointed pursuant to Article 3 of Chapter 160D "shall keep minutes of its proceedings"); 163-31(e) ("The county board of elections shall keep minutes recording all proceedings and findings at each of its meetings.").

18. Maready v. City of Winston-Salem, 342 N.C. 708, 733 (1996) (emphases in original) (internal quotation marks omitted).

19. *Id.*

20. G.S. 143-318.10(e). A separate statute appears to direct the county board of elections maintain its meeting minutes in written form. *Id.* § 163-31(e) (emphasis added) ("The minutes [of meetings of the board of elections] shall be recorded in a book which shall be kept in the board office[.]").

government records,[21] guidance promulgated by the Department of Natural and Cultural Resources pursuant to G.S. 132-8.2 may require local governments, within the limitations of funds available for the purpose, to create preservation duplicates of the minutes of some appointed board meetings in the form of paper or microfilm copies.[22] In light of this guidance, the best practice is for local appointed boards to keep written minutes of their meetings.

(b) Record of "Ayes" and "Noes." At the request of any member, the minutes shall indicate how each member voted by name on a particular matter.

> **Comment:** In general parliamentary practice, the minutes do not have to list how each member of a deliberative body voted on a motion unless the body has approved a member's request for a roll call vote.[23] Consistent with statutory rules for meetings of city councils and boards of county commissioners, Rule 6(b) makes the recording of the ayes and noes mandatory upon the request of any member, regardless of whether other members support the request.[24]

---

21. *See* GOV'T RECORDS SEC., N.C. DEP'T OF NAT. & CULTURAL RES., *General Records Schedule for Local Government Agencies,* Standard 1, Item 42 (Mar. 1, 2019) ("The official minutes of advisory boards may be destroyed only upon approval by the State Archives of North Carolina. The State Archives reserves the right to designate the minutes of any advisory board as permanent."), https://files.nc.gov/dncr-archives/documents/files/2019_local_standards_0.pdf.

22. GOV'T RECORDS BRANCH, N.C. DEP'T OF NAT. & CULTURAL RES., *Public Records Requiring Human-Readable Preservation Duplicates,* https://files.nc.gov/dncr-archives/documents/files/humreadabledupspolicy.pdf.

23. See *RONR* (11th ed.), p. 479, ll. 31–33 ("[W]hen the voting is by roll call, the names of those voting on each side . . . should be entered.").

24. *See* G.S. 153A-42 ("The clerk shall record the results of each vote in the minutes; and upon the request of any member of the board [of county commissioners], the ayes and noes upon any question shall be taken and recorded."); 160A-72 ("The results of each vote shall be recorded in the minutes, and upon the request of any member of the council, the ayes and noes upon any question shall be taken.").

(c) General Accounts of Closed Sessions. In addition to minutes, the board shall keep a general account of each closed session. The general account shall be sufficiently detailed to provide a person not in attendance with a reasonable understanding of what transpired. The board may combine the minutes and general account of a closed session into one document, so long as the document contains both a complete record of actions taken and the level of detail required for a general account.

> **Comment:** According to the open meetings law, "[w]hen a public body meets in closed session, it shall keep a general account of the closed session so that a person not in attendance would have a reasonable understanding of what transpired."[25] This wording plainly demands more than a mere record of actions taken.[26] Concerns about whether the general account of a particular closed session is sufficiently thorough should be referred to legal counsel.
>
> As paragraph (c) of this rule recognizes, it is common for local government boards, appointed and elected, to incorporate the minutes and general account of a closed session into a single record. There is no legal problem with that practice, so long as the record includes any actions taken by the board in closed session and enough information about what was discussed to satisfy the statutory standard for a general account.

(d) Sealing Closed-Session Records. Minutes and general accounts of closed sessions shall be sealed until unsealed by order of the board or in accordance with instructions adopted by competent authority. The sealed minutes and general account of any closed session may be withheld from public inspection, so long as public inspection would frustrate the purpose(s) of the closed session.

> **Comment:** Although the open meetings law allows a public body to withhold the minutes and general account of a closed

---

25. G.S. 143-318.10(e).

26. For an analysis of case law on the level of detail necessary for a general account, see Allen, *supra* note 17, at 2–4.

session from public inspection for as long as necessary to avoid frustrating the purpose of the closed session,[27] the state's public records law presumes that documents made or received in the transaction of public business must be made available for inspection and copying. The board therefore should not assume that closed session records are automatically sealed without action on its part.[28] By adopting Rule 6(d), the board decides that all of its closed session records will be sealed initially and remain so until they are unsealed by the board or in accordance with instructions adopted by competent authority, which could be the board itself or the governing board of the city, county, or other local government unit(s) to which the board belongs.

Rule 7. Broadcasting and Recording Meetings

(a) Right to Broadcast and Record. Any person may photograph, film, tape-record, or otherwise reproduce any part of a board meeting that must take place in open session. Except as provided in paragraph (c) of this rule, any radio or television station may broadcast any such part of a board meeting.

> **Comment:** Rule 7(a) restates G.S. 143-318.14(a).

(b) Advance Notice. Any radio or television station that plans to broadcast any portion of a board meeting shall so notify [_____] no later than [twenty-four hours] before the meeting. The failure to provide notice is not, by itself, grounds for preventing the broadcast of a board meeting.

> **Comment:** Rule 7(b) assumes that, if provided with advance notice of a broadcast media organization's intent to cover a board meeting, the board or local government staff members will be better able to accommodate the organization and minimize any interference with the meeting. In many places, the city or county clerk would be the appropriate

---

27. G.S. 143-318.10(e).
28. *See* David M. Lawrence, Public Records Law for North Carolina Local Governments 350 (2d ed. 2009).

individual to receive such notice. The last sentence in Rule 7(b) acknowledges that a media organization's failure to give the prescribed notice is not, by itself, a legal basis for refusing to allow the organization to broadcast a meeting.

(c) Equipment Placement. The board chair or an appropriate staff member may regulate the placement and use of camera or recording equipment in order to prevent undue interference with a board meeting, so long as he or she allows the equipment to be placed where it can carry out its intended function. If the board chair or staff member determines in good faith that the equipment and personnel necessary to broadcast, photograph, or record the meeting cannot be accommodated without undue interference to the meeting, and an adequate alternative meeting room is not readily available, the chair or staff member may require the pooling of the equipment and the personnel operating it.

> **Comment:** The open meetings law gives public bodies the authority to regulate the placement of cameras and recording equipment for the purpose of preventing undue interference with their meetings.[29] Rule 7(c) delegates that authority to the board chair or an appropriate staff member, primarily because, unlike the board, the chair or staff member may act outside of, and in advance of, a meeting.
>
> The open meetings law prohibits a public body from classifying the ordinary use of camera or recording equipment as an undue interference with its meeting.[30]

(d) Alternative Meeting Site. If the news media request an alternative meeting site to accommodate news coverage, and the board grants the request, the news media making the request shall pay the costs incurred by the local government unit in securing an alternative meeting site.

> **Comment:** Rule 7(d) tracks G.S. 143-318.14(b).

---

29. *See* G.S. 143-318.14(b).
30. *Id.*

Part IV. Organization of the Board

Rule 8. Organizational Meeting[; Selection of Chair] [and Vice Chair]

On the date and at the time of [the first regular meeting] in [July], all newly appointed and reappointed members of the board shall take and subscribe the oath of office as the first order of new business. [As the second order of new business, the board shall elect a chair [and vice chair].]

> **Comment:** It is common for local government appointed boards to hold organizational meetings annually. Ordinarily these meetings are timed to follow the appointment or reappointment of members. Statutes control the timing of some organizational meetings, and a board subject to such a law will need to adopt a version of Rule 8 that conforms to the statutory language.[31]

Organizational Meeting Business

Two important things happen at most organizational meetings: (1) new members and reappointed members take and subscribe the oath of office, and (2) the board selects the presiding officer, unless the presiding officer is selected in another way, such as by the city council or board of county commissioners. If the

---

31. G.S. 63-81(c) ("The [special airport] district board shall elect annually in January from among its members a chairman, vice-chairman, secretary and treasurer."); 105-322(e) (county board of equalization and review to hold its first meeting of each year "not earlier than the first Monday in April and not later than the first Monday in May"); 153A-425 (initial organizational meeting of regional solid waste management authority to occur "at such time and place as is agreed upon by its member units of local government"); 156-81(b) ("Immediately after the appointment of the board of drainage [district] commissioners, the clerk of the court of the county wherein such drainage proceeding is pending shall notify each of the commissioners in writing to appear at a certain time and place within the district and organize."); 158-9 (economic development commission to meet "promptly" following its appointment); 158-21 (county industrial development commission to hold first meeting within thirty days of its appointment); 160A-479.5 (initial organizational meeting of regional sports authority to happen "at a time and place agreed upon by its member governments"); 163-31(a) (organizational meeting of county board of elections must take place "at the courthouse or board office at noon on the Tuesday following the third Monday in July in the year of their appointment").

board has a vice chair, he or she should be designated at the organizational meeting, again unless another selection method is employed.

Oath of Office. Article VI, Section 7 of the North Carolina Constitution requires anyone elected or appointed to public office in this state to take and subscribe—that is, swear (or affirm) and sign—the oath prescribed therein before entering upon the duties of the office. This requirement is echoed in statutes mandating that everyone elected or appointed to city or county office take the oath.[32] Other statutes impose oath requirements on persons appointed to specific local government boards.[33]

General Statute 11-7 sets out an oath of office that all state and local elected and appointed officials must take and subscribe before they enter into or take up the duties of their offices. That oath substantially resembles the oath in Article VI, Section 7, and decisions from the North Carolina Supreme

32. G.S. 153A-26 (everyone elected or appointed to county office to take and subscribe constitutional oath); 160A-61 (same for everyone elected or appointed to city office).

33. G.S. 63-81(a) (oath of office mandatory for appointees to special airport district; oaths to be filed in minutes of the respective participating units of local government); 105-322(c) (oath of office mandatory for appointees to board of equalization and review); 130A-354(c) (setting out oath of office for members of mosquito control district board); 143B-1253 (oath of office mandatory for members of veterans' recreation authority); 157-35 (oath of office mandatory for appointees to regional housing authority); 159B-9(c) (same for members and alternate members of joint municipal electric power agency); 159B-43(c) (same for members of joint municipal assistance agency); 159C-4(a) (same for members of county industrial facilities and pollution authority); 160D-309 (same for appointees to planning boards, boards of adjustment, historic preservation commissions, appearance commissions, housing appeals boards, and other advisory boards established pursuant to Article 3 of G.S. Chapter 160D); 162A-5(c) (same for appointees to water and sewer authority); 162A-34(a) (same for appointees to metropolitan water district board); 162A-67(d) (same for appointees to metropolitan sewerage district board); 162A-85.3(d) (same for appointees to metropolitan water and sewerage district); 163-30(e) (same for appointees to county boards of elections).

Court and the North Carolina Court of Appeals imply that taking either oath is equivalent to taking the other.[34]

General Statute 11-11 prescribes additional oaths for designated local government officials.[35] The statute also has a general oath for county officers not covered by its position-specific provisions, a category that encompasses anyone appointed to a county board if a seat on that board constitutes a public office. There is no subscription requirement in G.S. 11-11, so an individual does not have to sign any oath taken under that statute.

Other statutes contain wording requirements for the oaths taken by appointees to certain local government boards.[36]

The state constitution does not explain what constitutes a public office. While elected board members clearly hold public offices, the courts have developed criteria for determining which appointed positions in state and local government qualify as public offices under the state constitution. For an appointed position to constitute a public office, it must (1) be created by state law, (2) exercise the sovereign power of the state, and (3) involve significant discretionary authority.[37] Many local government appointed boards either are not created by state law or are purely advisory in nature. Strictly speaking, the oath requirements in Article VI, Section 7, G.S. 11-7, and G.S. 11-11 likely do not apply to their members. (A separate law directs appointees to zoning-related advisory boards to

---

34. The cases referred to are *Baxter v. Nicholson*, 363 N.C. 829 (2010) and *State v. Sullivan*, 201 N.C. App. 540 (2009), which are discussed in Trey Allen, *One Oath or Two? What is THE Oath of Office?* Coates' Canons: NC Loc. Gov't L. Blog (Jan. 27, 2017), http://canons.sog.unc.edu/one-oath-or-two-what-is-the-oath-of-office.

35. Police officers are the only city officials who fall under one of the position-specific oaths found in G.S. 11-11.

36. G.S. 105-322(c) (additional language to be added to oath taken by persons appointed to boards of equalization and review); 163-30(e) (wording of oath to be taken by persons appointed to county boards of elections).

37. A. Fleming Bell, II, Ethics, Conflicts, and Offices: A Guide for Local Officials 131 (2d ed. 2010).

take the constitutional oath anyway.[38]) Nonetheless, because negative legal consequences can flow from a person's wrongful failure to take and subscribe the oath, Rule 8 errs on the side of having new and returning board members take and subscribe the oath.[39]

Only certain officials may administer the oath of office.[40] They include, among others, mayors, chairs of boards of county commissioners, city and county clerks, and notaries public. Deputy city and county clerks, if sworn, may administer the oath.[41]

Selection of Chair and Other Officers. State law expressly vests some local government appointed boards with the power to select their presiding officers.[42] It obliges city and county

---

38. Anyone appointed to an advisory board established pursuant to G.S. Chapter 160D, Article 3, must take the oath of office. G.S. 160D-309.

39. Under G.S. 14-229, an individual who undertakes the duties of a public office without first taking, subscribing, and filing the oath of office is guilty of a Class 1 misdemeanor. Similarly, G.S. 128-5 provides that any person who enters upon the duties of a public office without first taking the oath of office shall be subject to a forfeiture of $500 (to be used for the poor of the county). Both statutes authorize ejectment from office.

40. G.S. 11-7.1.

41. G.S. 11-8.

42. G.S. 63-81(c) ("The [special airport] district board shall elect annually in January from among its members a chairman[.]"); 108A-7 ("[The county board of social services] shall elect a chairman from its members at its July meeting each year, and the chairman shall serve a term of one year or until a new chairman is elected by the board."); 108A-15.8(g) ("A chairperson shall be elected annually by a regional board of social services."); 122C-119(b) ("Members of the area [authority] board elect the board's chairman."); 130A-35(e) ("A chairperson shall be elected annually by a county board of health."); 130A-37(f) (same for district board of health); 130A-45.1(h) (same for public health authority board."); 130A-354(c) (mosquito control district board to appoint its chair); 131E-18(c) (mayor or chair of board of county commissioners selects first chair of hospital authority board; hospital authority board members select subsequent chairs from among themselves); 143B-1254 ("When the office of the first chairman of the [veterans' recreation] authority becomes vacant, the authority shall select a chairman from among its members."); 153A-77(c) ("A chairperson shall be elected annually by the members of the consolidated human services board."); 153A-266 (city or county library board of trustees "shall elect a chairman and may elect other officers"); 153A-394 (regional planning commission to organize "by electing a chairman and any other officers

governing bodies or other officials to appoint the presiding
officers of a few appointed boards, though in some cases that
authority extends only to the appointment of the board's first
presiding officer.[43] Where state law is silent, the city council or
board of county commissioners is free to decide the method for

that the resolution specifies or that the commission considers advisable");
153A-425 ("The governing board of a regional solid waste management authority
shall hold an initial organizational meeting . . . and shall elect a chairman[.]");
157-5(e) ("When the office of the first chair of [a city or county housing] authority
becomes vacant, the authority shall select a chair from among its members.");
157-36(k) ("The commissioners of a regional housing authority shall elect a chair
from among the commissioners[.]"); 158-9 ("Upon its appointment, the economic
development commission shall promptly meet and elect from among its members
a chairman and such other officers as it may choose[.]"); 158-21 (county industrial
development commission to appoint chair from its membership); 159B-9(d) (The
board of commissioners of the joint [municipal electric power] agency shall
annually elect one of the commissioners as chairman[.]"); 159B-43(d) ("The board
of commissioners of the joint municipal assistance agency shall annually elect one
of the commissioners as president[.]"); 159C-4(c) ("The board of commissioners
of the [county industrial facilities and pollution control financing] authority shall
annually elect from its membership a chairman[.]"); 160A-510 ("The members of a
[redevelopment] commission shall select from among themselves a chairman[.]");
160A-553 ("When the office of the first chairman of the [parking] authority
becomes vacant, the authority shall select a chairman from among its members.");
160A-577 ("The members of the [public transportation] authority shall elect a
chairman . . . from the membership of the authority."); 160A-605(e) (same for
regional public transportation authority); 160A-664(d) (same for regional natural
gas district board); 162A-5(c) (same for water and sewer authority); 162-34(a) (same
for metropolitan water district board); 162A-67(d) (same for metropolitan sewerage
district board); 162A-85.3(e) (same for metropolitan water and sewerage district
board).

43. G.S. 18B-700(b), (c) (governing body to appoint chair of local ABC board);
105-322(a) ("The board of [county] commissioners shall also designate the chairman
of the [board of equalization and review]."); 131E-18(c) ("The mayor or the chairman
of the county board of commissioners shall name the first chair of the [city or
county hospital] authority."); 143-1254 (mayor to appoint first chair of veterans'
recreation authority); 156-81 (clerk of court to appoint chair of drainage district
board); 157-5(a) (mayor to designate housing authority's first chair; subsequent
chairs to be selected by authority from among its members); 160A-553 ("[T]he
city council shall designate the [parking authority's] first chairman."); 163-30(a)
(Governor to name chair of county board of elections).

selecting board chairs. Otherwise a local government appointed board may determine how and when its chair will be chosen.

It is usually a good idea to have a vice chair whose job is to run meetings in the chair's absence. For some appointed boards, the appointment of a vice chair is required by statute.[44]

State law requires some local government appointed boards to select additional officers. For example, in addition to having a chair and vice chair, a public transportation authority must have a secretary, who may or may not be a member of the authority.[45]

---

44. G.S. 63-81(c) ("The [special airport] district board shall elect annually in January from among its members a . . . vice-chairman[.]") 130A-354(c) (mosquito control district board to appoint vice chair); 131E-18(c) (city or county hospital authority to select vice chair); 143B-1254 (same for veterans' recreation authority); 157-5(e) (same for housing authority); 158-21 (same for county industrial commission); 159B-9(d) (same for joint municipal electric power agency); 159B-43(d) (joint municipal assistance agency annually to select one of its members as vice president); 159C-4(c) (county industrial facilities and pollution control financing authority annually to select one of its members as vice chair); 160A-510 (redevelopment commission to select vice chair from among its members); 160A-553 (same for parking authority); 160A-577 (same for public transportation authority); 160A-605(e) (same for regional public transportation authority); 160A-664(d) (same for regional natural gas district board); 162A-5(c) (same for water and sewer authority); 162A-34(a) (same for metropolitan water district board); 162A-67(d) (same for metropolitan sewerage district board); 162A-85.3(d) (same for metropolitan water and sewerage district board).

45. G.S. 160A-577. See also id. §§ 63-81(c) (special airport district board to appoint annually from among its members a "secretary and treasurer"); 130A-354(c) (mosquito control district board to appoint "a secretary and a treasurer"); 158-21 (county industrial development commission to appoint "secretary and treasurer"); 159-B-9(d) (joint municipal electric power agency to appoint annually a secretary and treasurer); 159B-43(d) (same for joint municipal assistance agency); 159C-4(c) (same for county industrial facilities and pollution control financing authority); 160A-605(e) (same for public transportation authority); 160A-664(d) (same for regional natural gas district board); 162A-5(c) (water and sewer authority must select "a secretary and a treasurer who may but need not be members of the authority); 162A-67(d) (same for metropolitan sewerage district board); 162A-85.3(d) (same for metropolitan water and sewerage district board).

Part V. Types of Meetings

Rule 9. Regular Meetings

(a) **Regular Meeting Schedule.** The board [may][shall] annually adopt a regular-meeting schedule showing the time(s) and place(s) of its regular meetings for the year.

> **Comment:** State law requires some local government appointed boards to meet at designated intervals.[46] Others find it necessary to meet regularly because of the volume of business they have to conduct. Quite a few local government boards, though, do not need to meet on a regular basis. Boards in this last category may wish to refrain from adopting regular-meeting schedules and simply call special meetings whenever matters arise that demand their attention.

(b) **Notice of Regular Meeting Schedule.** The board shall ensure that a copy of its current regular meeting schedule, complete with the time and place of each regular meeting, is filed with [the clerk to the board of county commissioners] [the city clerk] [the board's clerk or secretary] and posted on the board's website, if there is one.

> **Comment:** The open meetings law mandates that local government boards provide two kinds of public notice of their regular meetings.

> *Filed Notice.* If a local government board belongs to a county government, its regular meeting schedule must be filed with the clerk to the board of county commissioners.

---

46. G.S. 108A-7 (county board of social services to meet "at least once per month, or more often if a meeting is called by the chairman"); 108A-15.8(k) (regional board of social services to meet "at least quarterly"); 122C-119(a) (area authority board to meet "at least six times per year"); 130A-35(i) (county board of health to meet "at least quarterly"); 130A-37(j) (same for district board of health); 130A-45.1(l) (same for public health authority board); 130A-354(c) (same for mosquito control district board); 139-41(b) (same for county watershed improvement commission); 153A-77(c) (same for consolidated human services board); 156-81(f) (drainage district board to meet "once each month . . . during the progress of drainage construction, and more often if necessary"); 158-9 (economic development commission to meet regularly, "at least once every three months, at places and dates specified in the rules").

If the board belongs to a city government, its regular meeting schedule must be filed with the city clerk. If the board belongs to neither kind of government, its regular meeting schedule must be filed with the board's own clerk or secretary or, if the board has no clerk or secretary, with the clerk to the board of county commissioners in the county where the board normally meets.[47]

Online Notice. If a public body has a website, it must ensure that its regular-meeting schedule is posted there.[48]

(c) Change to Regular Meeting Schedule. The board may revise its regular-meeting schedule to change the time or place of a particular regular meeting or all regular meetings within a specified period. The board shall ensure that the revised regular meeting schedule is filed with the [the clerk to the board of county commissioners] [the city clerk] [the board's clerk or secretary] at least seven calendar days before the first meeting held pursuant to the revised schedule. The board shall also have the revised schedule posted on the board's website, if there is one.

> **Comment:** The seven-day filing requirement comes from the open meetings law.[49]

Rule 10. Special Meetings

(a) Calling Special Meetings. The chair [or a majority of the members] may call a special meeting of the board. Alternatively, a special meeting may be called by vote of the board in open session during a regular meeting or another duly called special meeting.

> **Comment:** The open meetings law says nothing about who may call special meetings of public bodies. For the most part, local government appointed boards may decide this matter

---

47. G.S. 143-318.12(a).
48. G.S. 143-318.12(d).
49. G.S. 143-318.12(a).

for themselves, though in some instances the matter is governed in statute.[50]

(b) Notice to the Public. At least forty-eight hours before a special meeting, the board shall cause written notice of the meeting's date, time, place, and purpose(s) to be (1) posted on the board's principal bulletin board or, if the board has no such bulletin board, at the door of the board's usual meeting room and (2) delivered, emailed, or mailed to each newspaper, wire service, radio station, television station, and person who has filed a written request for notice with [the board's clerk] [the board's secretary] [a person designated by the board]. If the board has a website maintained by one or more of its employees, the board shall also have the notice posted there prior to the special meeting.

> **Comment:** Rule 10(b) restates the open meetings law's public notice requirements for special meetings.[51] The law is silent concerning whether, or under what circumstances, a public body may take up items not listed in the notice. "Perhaps the silence of the open meetings law indicates that the statement of purpose, at least if made in good faith, does not limit

---

50. For several local government appointed boards, the rule is that the chair or any three members may call a special meeting. G.S. 108A-15.8 (regional social services board); 122C-119(b) (area authority); 130A-35(i) (county board of health); 130A-37(j) (district board of health); 130A-45.1(l) (public health authority board); 153A-77(c) (consolidated human services board); 163-31(c) (county board of elections). For others, the rules are slightly different. G.S. 63-81(b) ("Special meetings [of the special airport district] may be called by the chairman on his own initiative and shall be called by him upon request of two or more members of the board. All members shall be notified in writing at least 24 hours in advance of such meeting."); 108A-7 (chair may call special meeting of county social services board); 130A-354(c) (chair or any two members may call special meeting of mosquito control district board); 139-41(b) (chair "or any member" may call special meeting of county watershed commission); 156-81(f) (chair may call special meeting of drainage district board and must call special meeting "upon the written request of the owners of a majority in area of the land in the district"); 162A-34(a) (special meeting of metropolitan water district "may be called by the chairman on his own initiative and shall be called by him upon request or two or more members"); 162A-67(d) (same for metropolitan sewerage district board).
51. G.S. 143-318.12(b)(2), (e).

discussion of or action on other topics. A public body should be careful about going beyond the notice, however. Appellate courts in some other states (although not all) have found violations of their open meetings laws when items not in the notice were discussed and acted upon."[52]

(c) Notice to Members. If the chair [or a majority of the members] called the special meeting, [the chair] [whoever called the meeting] shall ensure that notice of the meeting's date, time, place, and purpose(s) is mailed, emailed, or delivered to the other members at least forty-eight hours before the meeting. If the special meeting was called at another duly held meeting of the board, and one or more members were absent, the chair shall ensure that notice of the meeting's date, time, place, and purpose(s) is mailed, emailed, or delivered to any absent member(s) a minimum of forty-eight hours in advance of the special meeting.

> **Comment:** While the open meetings law does not specifically require written notice to the board members, such notice can help avoid questions about whether all board members knew of the meeting and had an opportunity to attend.[53] A board's actions may be subject to legal challenge if a special meeting is deliberately called in a manner that precludes participation by one or more members.

Rule 11. Emergency Meetings
(a) Calling Emergency Meetings. The chair [or a majority of the members] may call an emergency meeting of the board, but only when necessary to address generally unexpected circumstances that demand the board's immediate attention.

---

52. Frayda S. Bluestein & David M. Lawrence, Open Meetings and Local Governments in North Carolina: Some Questions and Answers 36–37 (8th ed. 2017).

53. Members of a mosquito control district board must receive at least three days' notice of a special meeting. G.S. 130A-354(c). In contrast, "[a]ll members [of a special airport district] shall be notified in writing at least 24 hours in advance of [a special] meeting." *Id.* § 63-81(b).

Comment: Rule 11(a) incorporates the open meetings law's standard for calling emergency meetings.[54]

(b) Notice of Emergency Meetings. Reasonable steps shall be taken by the chair [or the members who called the meeting] to notify other board members of an emergency meeting. Additionally, notice of the meeting shall be given to each local newspaper, local wire service, local radio station, and local television station that has filed with [the board's clerk] [the board's secretary] [a person designated by the board] a written request to be notified of emergency meetings. To be valid, the request must include the newspaper's, wire service's, or station's telephone number. Notice may be given by telephone, email, or the same method used to notify board members. Notice shall be provided immediately after members have been notified and at the expense of the media organization notified.

Comment: The open meetings law says nothing about providing emergency-meeting notification to the members of a public body. Recognizing that the precise nature of an emergency could make some notification methods impracticable, Rule 11(b) simply directs that members receive reasonable notice of an emergency meeting. The provisions regarding notice to media organizations are taken from the open meetings law.[55]

(c) Transaction of Other Business Prohibited. Only business connected with the emergency may be considered at an emergency meeting.

Comment: Rule 11(c) reflects the open meetings law's restriction on the transaction of business at emergency meetings.[56]

Rule 12. Recessed Meetings

(a) Calling Recessed Meetings. When conducting a properly called regular, special, or emergency meeting, the board may recess the meeting to another date, time, or place by a procedural

---

54. G.S. 143-318.12(f).
55. G.S. 143-318.12(b)(3).
56. *Id.*

motion made and adopted in open session, as provided in Rule 25 (Motion 3). The motion shall state the time (including the date, if the meeting will resume on a different day) and place at which the meeting will resume.

(b) Notice of Recessed Meetings. If the board's website is maintained by one or more board employees, notice of the recessed meeting's date, time, and place shall appear on the website prior to the meeting. No further notice of a properly called recessed meeting is required.

> **Comment:** This rule follows the open meetings law's requirements for recessed meetings.[57] The procedural mechanism for setting a recessed meeting is a motion to recess to a time and place certain (Rule 25, Motion 3).

Part VI. Agenda
Rule 13. Agenda
(a) Draft Agenda.

(1) *Preparation.* The board's [clerk] [secretary] [chief administrative officer] shall prepare a draft agenda for each meeting of the board.

(2) *Requesting placement of items on draft agenda.* Members may, by timely request, have items placed on the draft agenda for any regular meeting. Members shall submit their requests to the board's [clerk] [secretary] [chief administrative officer] at least [two] working days before the meeting date.

(3) *Supplemental information/materials.* A copy of all draft orders, policies, regulations, or resolutions shall be attached to the draft agenda. [The board's [clerk] [secretary] [chief administrative officer] shall prepare an agenda packet that includes, for each item of business listed on the draft agenda, as much background information on the topic as is available and feasible to reproduce.]

---

57. G.S. 143-318.12(b)(1), (e).

(4) *Delivery to board members.* Each member shall receive a copy of the draft agenda [and the agenda packet]. [Except in the case of an emergency meeting, the draft agenda [and the agenda packet] shall be provided to each member at least [twenty-four hours] before the meeting.]

(5) *Public inspection.* The draft agenda [and agenda packet, except for materials not subject to inspection or copying under the public records law,] shall be available to the public when [it is] [they are] ready to be circulated to members.

Comment: No statute requires local government boards to use agendas. Many boards do so anyway, primarily because agendas aid them in organizing meeting materials and in controlling the length of their meetings. Some boards also find agendas useful because, when provided to members in advance, they enhance members' meeting preparation.

Agenda Preparation/Materials. Rule 13(a)(1) describes a typical agenda-preparation process. It might need modification if the board employs another method.

Rule 13(a)(3) requires that longer or more complex proposals be reduced to writing and attached to the agenda, so that members will have a clear idea of what they are being asked to approve.

The second sentence in Rule 13(a)(4) should be added if members wish to receive meeting agendas and supporting documents in advance of each non-emergency meeting.

The Public Records Law and Agendas. There is uncertainty in the law over the point at which a draft agenda and agenda packet must be made available for inspection or copying in response to a public records request. The case law in North Carolina does not provide a clear answer to this question, but the safe approach—taken by Rule 13(a)(5)—seems to be to regard a draft agenda and agenda packet as public records as soon as they are ready for circulation.[58] The redaction or

---

58. *See* Lawrence, *supra* note 28, at 15 ("[A] court might exclude . . . a draft [that is still in a very preliminary form] from the definition of public record, at least until

omission of certain records may be necessary or permissible to the extent that the agenda packet contains confidential, privileged, or non-public records.

State law does not mandate that the board post draft agendas or agenda packets online. If the board posts draft agendas or agenda packets online in a format that allows a person to view and print or save them, there is no legal obligation to provide paper copies of the posted documents in response to public records requests.[59]

(b) Adoption of the Agenda

(1) *Adoption.* As its first order of business at each meeting, the board shall review the draft agenda, make whatever revisions it deems appropriate, and adopt the agenda for the meeting.

(2) *Amending the agenda.* Both before and after it adopts the agenda, the board may add or subtract agenda items by majority vote of the members present and voting, except when the board's consideration of new agenda items would violate state law or these rules.

(3) *Designation of items "For Discussion and Possible Action."* The board may designate an agenda item "For Discussion and Possible Action." The designation signifies that the board intends to discuss the item and may, if it so chooses, take action on the item following the discussion.

Comment: Although the board enjoys broad discretion in deciding what business to conduct at its meetings, state law imposes some limitations. Procedural requirements for certain undertakings prevent the board from taking some actions without warning. For instance, a local board of health may not adopt, amend, or repeal a local board of health rule without first providing the published notice specified in G.S. 130A-39(d).

---

the authority begins to circulate it to others, but there appears to be little other room for excluding from public access documents that are closer to completion.").

59. G.S. 132-6(a1).

The open meetings law can be another obstacle to the last-minute addition of agenda items. As explained in the *Comment* to Rule 10(b), the board runs some risk of violating the open meetings law if, at a special meeting, it takes up matters that did not appear in the public notice of the meeting. Similarly, as noted in the *Comment* to Rule 11(c), the open meetings law prohibits the board from taking up matters at an emergency meeting that are unconnected to the emergency.

It often happens that members want to discuss an issue informally, even when they are unsure about whether they will ultimately take action on the matter. Under Rule 13(b)(3), by designating particular agenda items "For Discussion and Possible Action," the board preserves the option of taking action if discussion leads to agreement on a course of action.

(c) Consent Agenda. The board may designate part of an agenda for a regular meeting as the consent agenda. The person(s) charged with preparing the draft agenda may place routine or non-controversial items on the consent agenda. Prior to approving the meeting agenda, the board must honor any member's request to move an item from the consent agenda to new or unfinished business. The board may approve all items on the consent agenda through the adoption of a single motion to that effect, but the minutes shall list each item so approved.

> **Comment:** The consent agenda groups together items that the individuals who prepare the draft agenda regard as non-controversial and routine. This procedural tool can improve efficiency by enabling the board to dispose of multiple matters with a single motion and vote.
>
> The board reviews the consent agenda during its examination of the draft agenda at the beginning of a meeting. Each member is free to ask for the removal of one or more items from the consent agenda. Such a request must be honored, and the item(s) in question considered separately as new or unfinished business. The board may

then approve the remaining items on the consent agenda simultaneously through the adoption of a single motion. For clarity's sake, the minutes should list each item approved by the board through its approval of the consent agenda.

Because the consent agenda is voted on at the outset of a meeting, items likely to generate significant public interest should not be placed on the consent agenda, especially when there will be an opportunity for public comment. If the board misuses the consent agenda to dispose of controversial as well as routine matters before the public can weigh in, members of the public may conclude that the board does not value their input.

(d) Informal Discussion of Agenda Items. The board may informally discuss an agenda item even when no motion regarding that item is pending.

> **Comment:** Standard parliamentary practice does not permit debate on a matter in the absence of a pending motion.[60] Small boards, though, can often benefit from informal discussion prior to the making of any motion. Indeed, *Robert's Rules of Order* expressly allows small boards to engage in informal discussion of an issue while no motion is pending.[61] Rule 13(d) follows *Robert's* on this point. If informal discussion results in a motion, debate on the motion should be conducted pursuant to Rule 26.

Rule 14. Acting by Reference to Agenda or Other Document

The board shall not deliberate, vote, or otherwise take action on any matter by reference to the agenda or any other document unless copies of the agenda or document are available for public inspection at the meeting and so worded that persons in attendance can understand what is being deliberated or acted upon.

> **Comment:** This rule incorporates the open meetings law's restrictions on acting by reference.[62]

---

60. *RONR* (11th ed.), p. 34, ll. 7–9.

61. *Id.* at 488, ll. 7–8.

62. G.S. 143-318.13(c).

Rule 15. Agenda Items from Members of the Public

If a member of the public wishes to request that the board include an item on its regular-meeting agenda, the individual shall submit the request in writing to the board's [clerk] [secretary] [chief administrative officer] at least [two] working days before the meeting date. The board is not obligated to place an item on the agenda merely because such a request has been received.

> **Comment:** While it is not unusual for members of the public to ask that an item be placed on the board's meeting agenda, generally the board has no legal obligation to honor such requests. The open meetings law guarantees the public's right to attend board meetings, but control of the agenda belongs to the board. Yet a total refusal to consider agenda requests from residents and other interested persons could lead to negative perceptions of the board. This rule creates a mechanism for the submission of agenda requests while plainly stating that the board may choose not to act on them.

Rule 16. Order of Business

Items shall be placed on a regular-meeting agenda according to the order of business. The usual order of business for each regular meeting shall be as follows:

- adoption of the agenda,
- approval of the consent agenda,
- approval of the previous meeting minutes,
- public hearings,
- public comment,
- administrative reports,
- committee reports,
- unfinished business, and
- new business.

Without objection, the chair may call agenda items in any order most convenient for the dispatch of business.

Comment: This rule's placement of public hearings and public comment ahead of reports and unfinished and new business allows members of the public to address the board without having to stay for the whole meeting. Likewise, by putting reports before old and new business, the suggested order of business may afford some staff members the option of leaving prior to adjournment.

For purposes of these rules, unfinished business consists of matters carried over from a previous meeting, either because the board adjourned without completing its order of business or because it adopted a motion postponing the matters until the present meeting.[63]

Part VII. Role of the Presiding Officer
Rule 17. The Chair
(a) Presiding Officer. The chair shall preside at meetings of the board.

(b) Voting by the Chair. [The chair has the same duty to vote as other members, though in no event may the chair break a tie on a motion on which he or she has already voted.] [The chair may vote only in the event of a tie.]

Comment: If the board adopts a version of Rule 29 that obliges members to vote except when excused for a valid reason, it will need to decide whether to extend that same duty to the chair. If the board instead opts to allow the chair to vote only in the event of a tie, it should omit the first bracketed sentence in Rule 17(b) in favor of the second. The chairs of a few local government appointed boards have a statutory right to vote on all questions.[64]

---

63. This motion would be made in accordance with Rule 25, Motion 9 (Motion to Postpone to a Certain Time).

64. G.S. 63-81(b) (chair of special airport district board entitled to vote); 162A-34(a) (same for metropolitan water district board); 162A-67(d) (same for metropolitan sewerage-district board); 162A-85.3(f) (same for metropolitan water and sewerage district board).

(c) Recognition of Members. A member must be recognized by the chair (or other presiding officer) in order to address the board, but recognition is not necessary for an appeal pursuant to Rule 25 (Motion 1).

> **Comment:** Standard parliamentary practice does not permit a member to address a body without being recognized by the presiding officer.[65] On the other hand, the presiding officer must recognize any member who seeks the floor and is entitled to it.[66] Moreover, under Rule 25 (Motion 1), if a member's purpose in seeking the floor is to appeal a procedural ruling by the chair, the member may make the appeal regardless of whether the chair recognizes the member. If recognition by the chair were necessary in that situation, the chair could defeat the appeal simply by refusing to call on the member.

(d) Powers as Presiding Officer. As presiding officer, the chair is to enforce these rules and maintain order and decorum during board meetings. To that end, the chair may

(1) rule on points of parliamentary procedure, to include ruling out of order any motion clearly offered for obstructive or dilatory purposes;

(2) determine whether a member or other speaker has gone beyond reasonable standards of courtesy in his or her remarks and entertain and rule on objections from other members on this ground;

(3) entertain and answer questions of parliamentary procedure;

(4) call a brief recess at any time; and

(5) adjourn in an emergency.

> **Comment:** The term "recess" is defined in *Robert's Rules of Order* as "a short intermission in the assembly's proceedings, commonly of only a few minutes, which does not close

---

65. *RONR* (11th ed.), p. 376, ll. 13–16.
66. *Id.* at 376, l. 16; 377, l. 1.

the meeting and after which business will immediately be resumed at exactly the point where it was interrupted."[67]

Rule 17(d)(4) allows the chair to call for a brief recess in the belief that members can sometimes benefit from a "cooling off" period, especially when contentious topics are under consideration.[68] Ideally, as presiding officer, the chair will be well placed to judge when a short break might help ease tensions at a meeting of the board.

When to adjourn is normally a decision for the board to make through a motion and vote, but Rule 17(d)(5) authorizes the chair to adjourn a board meeting "in an emergency." The equivalent provision in *Robert's* offers some guidance regarding the type of event that would justify an emergency adjournment by the chair: "In the event of a fire, riot, or other extreme emergency, if the chair believes taking time for a vote on adjourning would be dangerous to those present, he should declare the meeting adjourned[.]"[69]

(e) Appeals of Procedural Rulings. A member may appeal a decision made or an answer given by the chair under subparagraph (d)(1), (2), or (3) of this rule in accordance with Rule 25 (Motion 1).

Rule 18. Presiding Officer in the Chair's Absence

If the chair is absent, [the vice chair][another member designated by vote of the board] shall preside. [If both the chair and vice chair are absent, the board shall designate one of the members present to serve as temporary presiding officer.] Any member who presides in place of the chair has the powers listed in Rule 17(d). Service as presiding officer does not relieve a member of the [right to vote] [duty to vote on all questions except as excused from voting under Rule 29].

---

67. *Id.* at 230, ll. 20–23.

68. The chair's unilateral authority to call for a brief recess goes beyond the powers of presiding officers under *Robert's Rules of Order.* According to *Robert's,* a recess may be taken only on a motion and vote by the members, except when a recess is provided for in the meeting agenda. *Id.* § 20, pp. 230–33.

69. *Id.* at 86, ll. 26–29.

Comment: The board's word choices for Rule 18 will depend on whether the board (1) elects a vice chair and (2) imposes a duty to vote on its members.

Rule 19. When the Presiding Officer Is Active in Debate

If the chair or other presiding officer becomes active in the debate on a matter, he or she [may][shall] designate another member to preside over the debate.

Comment: In deciding whether the presiding officer *must* relinquish the gavel if he or she joins in debate, the board should remember that, when it comes to presiding officers, good leadership depends, to a certain degree, on not taking sides. If the presiding officer takes a position in debate, members on the other side of the issue might suspect that any procedural rulings detrimental to their cause result more from a desire to promote a certain outcome than from the impartial application of parliamentary principles. Yet on a small board, it may not always be feasible or even desirable for the presiding officer to withhold his or her views. If the board concludes that the presiding officer should be able, at least on some occasions, to participate in debate while still wielding the gavel, it should adopt the "may" option in Rule 19.

Part VIII. Motions and Voting

Rule 20. Action by the Board

Except as otherwise provided in Rules 28, 30, and 33, the board shall act by motion. Any member [other than the chair] may make a motion.

Comment: There are three situations in which these rules empower the board to act by procedural mechanisms other than a motion and vote. Rule 28 provides that a member's request to change his or her vote may be granted by unanimous consent in certain situations. Rule 30 permits the board to determine by unanimous consent that it will vote on a pending motion by written ballot. Rule 33 directs the board to act by nomination rather than by motion when filling vacancies on the board or on appointed bodies. When there is only one nominee, Rule 33 allows the board to approve the nomination by unanimous consent.

Members need not actually cast votes to grant a request for unanimous consent. The presiding officer may simply ask whether there is any objection and, hearing none, pronounce the request approved.[70]

If the chair has the same right to vote as other members, he or she should also be allowed to make motions. The chair probably should not make motions if he or she may vote only in the event of a tie. Traditionally, if the chair wants another board member to offer a particular motion, the chair will say something like: "The Chair will entertain a motion that . . . ."

Rule 21. Second Not Required

No second is required on any motion.

> **Comment:** It is standard parliamentary practice to refuse to entertain any motion that does not receive a second. The purpose of requiring a second "is to prevent time from being consumed by the assembly's having to dispose of a motion that only one person wants to see introduced."[71] This rationale makes sense as applied to large bodies. It would be grossly inefficient for a 100-member body to debate a motion that not one of its members is willing to second. This reasoning is not persuasive as to small boards, where even a single member constitutes a significant percentage of a board's total membership. The limited utility of seconds in the case of small boards is acknowledged by *Robert's Rules of Order*, which recommends that small boards not require seconds for motions.[72]

---

70. *Id.* at 54, ll. 13–29.
71. *Id.* at 36, ll. 28–31.
72. *Id.* at 488, l. 1.

Rule 22. One Motion at a Time

A member may make only one motion at a time.

> **Comment:** "The purpose of meeting procedures is to allow members to reach informed . . . decisions in an effective, efficient, orderly, courteous, and fair manner."[73] Allowing members to make more than one motion at a time would undermine that purpose by creating enormous potential for confusion.

Rule 23. Withdrawal of Motion

The member who introduces a motion may withdraw the motion unless the motion has been amended or put to a vote.

> **Comment:** Under *Robert's Rules of Order*, the member who makes a motion may withdraw it without anyone's consent until the presiding officer states the motion.[74] Once the motion has been stated by the presiding officer, ownership of the motion transfers to the body, and the member may not withdraw it without the body's consent.[75] The *Robert's* approach seems unduly restrictive for small boards, so this rule permits the member who made a motion to withdraw it unless the board has made the motion its own by amending it or the presiding officer has called for a vote on the motion.

Rule 24. Substantive (or Main) Motions

A substantive motion is not in order when any other motion is pending. Once the board disposes of a substantive motion, it may not take up a motion that presents essentially the same issue at the same meeting unless it first adopts a motion to reconsider pursuant to Rule 25 (Motion 13).

> **Comment:** A substantive motion is one that brings business before the board, such as a motion that the planning board recommend approval of a proposed zoning-ordinance

---

73. AMERICAN INSTITUTE OF PARLIAMENTARIANS STANDARD CODE OF PARLIAMENTARY PROCEDURE 2 (2012).

74. *RONR* (11th ed.), p. 295, ll. 31–33.

75. *Id.* at 296, ll. 21–25.

amendment.[76] A substantive motion may propose any action within the board's legal authority. Moreover, because Rule 20 requires the board to proceed by motion, a substantive motion is typically the only way the board may take such action.

A foundational principle of parliamentary procedure is that only one substantive proposal may be considered at any one time.[77] This rule therefore prohibits the introduction of a substantive motion while another motion is pending.

To promote efficiency, and consistent with *Robert's*, this rule also generally prevents the board from revisiting the subject matter of a substantive motion during the same meeting at which the motion was adopted or defeated.[78] The exception is when the board adopts a motion to reconsider the substantive motion, as provided in Rule 25 (Motion 13).

Rule 25. Procedural Motions

(a) Certain Motions Allowed. The board may consider only those procedural motions listed in this rule. Unless otherwise noted, each procedural motion may be debated and amended and requires a majority of votes cast, a quorum being present, for adoption.

> **Comment:** For purposes of these rules, a procedural motion is any non-substantive motion. Most procedural motions, if adopted, act on a substantive motion in some way, such as a motion to postpone the board's consideration of a substantive motion until its next regular meeting.
>
> The array of motions in *Robert's Rules of Order* that would qualify as procedural motions under these rules could prove bewildering. This rule retains only those procedural

---

76. *Id.* at 100, ll. 3–4 ("[A] *main motion* is a motion whose introduction brings business before the assembly[.]"). There is no mention in *Robert's Rules of Order* of "substantive motions" as such; the equivalent term in *Robert's* is "main motion." *See generally id.* § 10 (describing characteristics of a main motion).

77. *See id.* at 100, ll. 4–5 (noting that a main motion "can be made only when no other motion is pending.").

78. *See id.* at 111, ll. 11–15 (observing that typically "[n]o main motion is in order that presents substantially the same question as a motion that was finally disposed of earlier in the same session").

motions that seem likely to aid the board in its conduct of business, and many of them have been modified to make them more user-friendly.

Several of the procedural motions in *Robert's* are not subject to debate, which makes sense in that *Robert's* was written primarily with large assemblies in mind.[79] Valid concerns about efficiency can justify a large assembly's decision not to afford every member the right to speak on any and all motions. These rules favor debate on all motions, however, because (1) the board's small size makes extended debate on most procedural motions unlikely and (2) procedural mechanisms such as Motion 8 (below) can bring debate to a close if it becomes too time-consuming.

(b) Priority of Motions. The procedural motions set out in this paragraph are listed in order of priority. A procedural motion is not in order so long as another procedural motion of higher priority is pending, except that

- any procedural motion other than an appeal under Motion 1 is subject to amendment as provided in Motion 11 and
- a motion to call the question (end debate) may be made with regard to any procedural motion in accordance with Motion 8.

When several procedural motions are pending, voting shall begin with the procedural motion highest in priority, except that a motion to amend or end debate on the highest-priority motion shall be voted on first.

> **Comment:** As in *Robert's*, here the order of priority establishes which procedural motion yields to which—that is, which procedural motions may be made and considered while another procedural motion is pending.[80]
>
> Appendix B summarizes in table form the procedural motions described in this rule.

---

79. Under *Robert's*, for example, a motion to suspend the rules is not debatable. *Id.* at 261, l. 12.

80. *See generally id.* at 61, ll. 11–35; 62, ll. 1–10 (explaining *RONR*'s basic approach to ranking motions).

Motion 1. To Appeal a Ruling of the Presiding Officer. Any member may appeal the presiding officer's ruling on whether a motion is in order or on whether a speaker has violated reasonable standards of courtesy. The presiding officer's response to a question of parliamentary procedure may also be appealed by any member. An appeal is in order immediately after the disputed ruling or parliamentary response and at no other time. The member who moves to appeal need not be recognized by the presiding officer, and if timely made, the motion may not be ruled out of order.

> **Comment:** Rule 17(e) recognizes that members may appeal the presiding officer's rulings on most procedural matters and answers to questions of parliamentary procedure. Motion 1 is the vehicle for such an appeal. It is accorded the highest priority among procedural motions, in part because it is untimely if not made immediately. Another reason for ranking it first among procedural motions is to ensure that rulings on all other procedural motions are subject to appeal.

Motion 2. To Adjourn. This motion may be used to close a meeting. It is not in order if the board is in closed session.

> **Comment:** Unlike the motion to adjourn described in *Robert's*, this motion is debatable and amendable.[81] Like the *Robert's* motion to adjourn, this motion may interrupt deliberation on a pending matter.[82] Why should the board be allowed to adjourn when business is pending? Because a vote to adjourn in such circumstances would signal that the board is not prepared to take action on one or more pending matters, and these rules disfavor forcing the board to act before it is ready.

---

81. *Id.* at 236, ll. 7–8.
82. *Id.* at 233, ll. 17–33.

Motion 3. To Recess to a Time and Place Certain. This motion may be used to call a recessed meeting as permitted under Rule 12. The motion must state the time (including the date, if the meeting will reconvene on a different day) and place at which the meeting will resume. The motion is not in order if the board is in closed session.

> **Comment:** This motion is analogous to the motion to fix the time for an adjourned meeting in *Robert's*, though, unlike that motion, this motion is debatable.[83] In deference to the open meetings law, which allows a public body to "recess[] a regular, special, or emergency meeting" to another "time and place," these rules employ the term "recessed meeting" instead of "adjourned meeting."[84]

Motion 4. To Take a Brief Recess.

> **Comment:** This motion allows the board to pause a meeting for a few minutes. It should not be confused with a motion to recess to a time and place certain under Motion 3. In contrast to *Robert's*, these rules allow debate on a motion to take a brief recess.[85] If debate on the motion becomes prolonged, the chair may render both the motion and the debate moot by unilaterally recessing the meeting for a short time pursuant to Rule 17(d)(4).

Motion 5. To Follow the Agenda. This motion must be made at the time an item of business that deviates from the agenda is considered; otherwise, the motion is out of order as to that item.

> **Comment:** This motion is loosely patterned on the call for the orders of the day in *Robert's*, though unlike a call for the orders of the day, a motion to follow the agenda is debatable.[86] If adopted, it curtails the chair's freedom under Rule 16 to call agenda items out of order. If the board as

---

83. *See generally id.* § 22, pp. 242–46 (outlining the chief characteristics of a motion to fix the time to which to adjourn).

84. G.S. 143-318.12(b)(1).

85. *RONR* (11th ed.), p. 231, l. 30.

86. *See generally id.* at 219, ll. 1–20; 220, ll. 1–35; 221, ll. 1–18 (discussing key features of the call for the orders of the day).

a whole does not object to the deviation from the agenda, it may simply vote down the motion. Alternatively, the board may pass the motion but then amend the agenda in accordance with Rule 13(b)(2).

Motion 6. To Suspend the Rules. To be adopted, a motion to suspend the rules must receive affirmative votes equal to two-thirds of the board's actual membership, excluding any vacant seats. The board may not suspend provisions in these rules that restate state law requirements.

> **Comment:** This motion is generally the same as the motion to suspend the rules in *Robert's*, except that it is debatable and amendable.[87] This motion is in order when the board wishes to take some action within its legal authority but one or more of these rules prevents it from doing so. For example, the board could use this motion in the middle of a regular meeting to allow consideration of a proposed policy change that is not on the agenda. (The board could reach the same result by amending the agenda to add the proposed policy change.)
>
> Some provisions in these rules incorporate requirements of state law and, therefore, may not lawfully be suspended. The board may not suspend the notice requirements for special meetings set out in Rule 10, for instance.
>
> A motion to suspend the rules fails unless it receives affirmative votes equal to at least two thirds of the board's membership, excluding vacant seats. The purpose of this elevated vote threshold is to discourage the board from departing from its rules in the ordinary course of business.

Motion 7. To Defer Consideration. The board may defer its consideration of a substantive motion, and any proposed amendments thereto, to an unspecified time. A motion that has been deferred expires unless the board votes to revive it pursuant to Motion 12 within [100] days of deferral. A new motion having the

---

87. *See generally id.* § 25, pp. 260–67 (describing characteristics of the motion to suspend the rules).

same effect as a deferred motion may not be introduced until the latter has expired.

Comment: This motion is a hybrid of two motions in *Robert's*: the motion to postpone indefinitely and the motion to lay on the table.[88] If adopted, a motion to postpone indefinitely effectively kills the pending substantive motion at which it takes aim, thereby enabling a deliberative body to defeat the substantive motion without actually voting on it.[89] In contrast, a motion to lay on the table allows a deliberative body to set aside a pending substantive motion temporarily when a matter demanding immediate attention arises.[90] The body may return to the tabled motion later through the adoption of a motion to remove from the table.[91]

Under these rules, the motion to defer consideration is the proper mechanism for killing a substantive motion indirectly or for delaying consideration of it temporarily. If the board's goal is to kill the substantive motion indirectly, it merely has to adopt a deferral motion and leave the substantive motion in limbo until the period during which a motion to revive consideration (Motion 12) would be in order elapses, at which time the substantive motion will automatically expire. If the objective is to put off consideration of the substantive motion temporarily, the

---

88. *See generally id.* § 11, pp. 126–30 (describing characteristics of the motion to postpone indefinitely); § 17, pp. 209–18 (setting out the rules that apply to a motion to lay on the table).

89. *Id.* at 126, ll. 4–9 ("*Postpone Indefinitely* is a motion that the assembly decline to take a position on the main question. Its adoption kills the main motion . . . and avoids a direct vote on the question. It is useful in disposing of a badly chosen main motion that cannot be either adopted or expressly rejected without possibly undesirable consequences.").

90. *Id.* at 209, ll. 26–30 ("The motion to *Lay on the Table* enables the assembly to lay the pending question aside temporarily when something else of immediate urgency has arisen or when something else needs to be addressed before consideration of the pending question is resumed[.]").

91. *Id.* at 300, ll. 3–5 ("The object of the motion to *Take from the Table* is to make pending again before the assembly a motion or a series of adhering motions that previously has been laid on the table[.]").

board may accomplish its goal by adopting a deferral motion and later voting within the prescribed number of days to revive consideration. Like a motion to postpone indefinitely and a motion to table, a motion to defer consideration may include both a pending substantive motion and any pending amendments thereto.

In general, the board may not consider a new substantive motion that would have the same effect as a deferred motion until the deadline for reviving the latter has passed. Of course, if the board is determined to take up the new motion while the deferred motion remains pending, it may do so under Motion 6 by voting to suspend its rules to allow consideration of the new motion.

The motion to defer consideration should be distinguished from Motion 9, which may be used to postpone consideration of a substantive motion to a designated time. A substantive motion that has been postponed to a certain time must be brought up again at the time specified. No motion to revive is needed.

Motion 8. To End Debate (Call the Previous Question). If adopted, this motion terminates debate on a pending motion, thereby bringing it to an immediate vote. This motion is not in order until every member has had an opportunity to speak once on the pending motion.

> **Comment:** Many people wrongly assume that a member may bring debate on a pending motion to a close simply by saying, "I call the question," or words to that effect. A body that allows a single member to end debate in that way offends the fundamental parliamentary principle of majority rule. If a majority of members want debate on a matter to continue, no single member should have the power to override their will. Furthermore, allowing a single member to decide when debate must end could infringe on the right of other members to participate equally in the debate.

Under both *Robert's* and these rules, the words "I call the question" amount to a motion to end debate on a pending matter.[92] If a member calls the question when more than one motion is pending, the presiding officer should ensure that the member specifies the motion(s) on which he or she would like debate to stop.

Motion 8 differs from the motion for the previous question in *Robert's* in three significant respects. First, it is debatable.[93] Second, whereas *Robert's* allows a member to call the question at almost any point during a debate, provided the member has been recognized, Motion 8 bars the calling of the question until every member has had a chance to speak at least once.[94] Third, *Robert's* requires a two-thirds majority to bring debate to a close, but a simple majority of votes cast is enough to end debate under these rules.[95]

Motion 9. To Postpone to a Certain Time. This motion may be employed to delay the board's consideration of a substantive motion, and any proposed amendments thereto, until a designated day, meeting, or hour. During the period of postponement, the board may not take up a new motion raising essentially the same issue without first suspending its rules pursuant to Motion 6.

---

92. *Id.* at 202, ll. 5–10.

93. *Id.* at 200, l. 1.

94. A member may not interrupt another member to move the previous question. *Id.* at 199, l. 30.

95. *See id.* at 200, ll. 24–30; 201, ll. 1–2 (noting that *Robert's* imposes a supermajority requirement on the motion for the previous question because otherwise "a temporary majority of only one vote could deny the remaining members all opportunity to discuss any measure that such a majority wished to adopt or kill"). The rationale in *Robert's* for requiring a supermajority to end debate does not apply here because Motion 9 is not in order until every board member has had the opportunity to speak at least once on the motion in question.

Comment: This motion is similar to the motion to postpone to a certain time (or definitely) in *Robert's*.[96] It allows the board to postpone consideration of a matter until a particular day, meeting, or hour. The motion is appropriate when the board needs more information or deliberations on the matter are likely to be lengthy.

This motion should be distinguished from the motion to defer consideration (Motion 7), which can postpone the board's consideration of a matter indefinitely.

Motion 10. To Refer a Motion to a Committee. The board may vote to refer a substantive motion to a committee for study and recommendations. While the substantive motion is pending before the committee, the board may not take up a new motion raising essentially the same issue without first suspending its rules pursuant to Motion 6. If the committee fails to report on the motion within [sixty] days of the referral date, the board shall take up the motion if asked to do so by the member who introduced it.

Comment: The analogous motion in *Robert's* does not grant the introducer of a proposal the power to force consideration of the proposal if the committee to which it has been referred fails to act.[97] By creating such a right, these rules make it harder for other board members to defeat a proposal by sending it to a committee that will just "sit" on it.

Motion 11. To Amend
(a) Germaneness. A motion to amend must concern the same subject matter as the motion it seeks to alter.

Comment: An amendment is germane if it *"in some way involve[s]* the same question that is raised by the motion to

---

96. *See generally id.* § 14, pp. 179–91 (setting out the rules applicable to a motion to postpone to a certain time (or definitely)).

97. Under *Robert's*, when a body wishes to take up a matter that it has previously referred to a committee, the adoption of a motion to discharge a committee is usually necessary. *Id.* at 310, ll. 31–33; 311, ll. 1–5.

which it is applied."[98] An amendment is not germane if it introduces a question that is unrelated to the one posed by the original motion, but "an amendment can be hostile to, or even defeat, the spirit of the original motion and still be germane."[99] Of course, if the intent is to defeat the original motion, the most efficient way to accomplish that objective is to vote against the original motion.

In *Robert's* a motion to amend by deleting and replacing much or all of the original motion is referred to as a "motion to substitute" and is governed by its own subset of procedures.[100] To avoid confusion, these rules require both major and minor changes to be proposed through a motion to amend.

If the member who made the original motion disapproves of a pending motion to amend, that member is free under Rule 23 to withdraw the original motion, so long as no other proposed amendment to the motion has been adopted. If the original motion is withdrawn, another member may put the same issue to the board in the form of a new motion.

(b) Limit on Number of Motions to Amend. When a motion to amend is under consideration, a motion to amend the amendment may be made; however, no more than one motion to amend and one motion to amend the amendment may be pending at the same time.

> **Comment:** Consistent with *Robert's*, and to reduce the likelihood of confusion, these rules allow only one motion to amend (primary amendment) and one motion to amend the amendment (secondary amendment) to be pending simultaneously.[101] Such amendments are voted on in reverse order; that is, the secondary amendment is voted on first. Once the secondary amendment has been disposed of,

---

98. *Id.* at 136, ll. 8–9 (emphasis in original).
99. *Id.* at 136, ll. 17–19.
100. *Id.* § 12, pp. 153–62.
101. *Id.* at 135, ll. 27–30.

another secondary amendment may be offered. The same is true for primary amendments.[102]

Motion 12. To Revive Consideration. The board may vote to revive consideration of any substantive motion that has been deferred pursuant to Motion 7, provided it does so within [100] days of its vote to defer consideration.

> **Comment:** This motion replaces the motion to take from the table in *Robert's*.[103] It has been renamed to make its connection with Motion 7 apparent. Unlike the motion to take from the table, this motion may be debated and amended.[104] If the motion to revive consideration of a deferred motion is not adopted within the prescribed number of days, the deferred motion expires, though at that point the same issue presented by the deferred motion could be reintroduced in the form of a new substantive motion. The number of days specified in Motion 7 and Motion 12 should be the same.

Motion 13. To Reconsider. The board may vote to reconsider its action on a matter, provided the motion to reconsider is made (1) at the same meeting during which the action to be reconsidered took place and (2) by a member who voted with the prevailing side. For purposes of this motion, "the same meeting" includes any continuation of a meeting through a motion to recess to a certain time and place (Motion 3). The motion is not in order if it interrupts the board's deliberation on a pending matter.

> **Comment:** The restrictions on who may move to reconsider and when a motion to reconsider may be offered correspond to limitations on the parallel motion in *Robert's*.[105]
> The "prevailing side" is usually the majority, but not always. Some actions require more than a simple majority for approval. If a motion to take such an action garners a

---

102. *Id.*
103. *See generally id.* § 34, pp. 300–04 (describing characteristics of the motion to take from the table).
104. *Id.* at 301, ll. 22–23.
105. *Id.* at 315, ll. 28–31; 316, ll. 22–26.

simple majority but not the necessary supermajority, the members who voted against the motion constitute the prevailing side, even though they were in the minority.[106] If a motion fails due to a tie vote, the members who voted against the motion are the prevailing side.

The limitation on when a motion to reconsider may be made should not be understood to stop the board from reversing itself at a subsequent meeting. In general, the board is free to undo an action taken at a prior meeting, except when reversal would violate the law.

The board may reverse an action taken at a previous meeting in either of two ways. It may pass a new motion that has the opposite effect of the one previously adopted. Alternatively, as permitted by Motion 14, the board may vote to rescind or repeal the prior action.

The motion to reconsider is allowed under these rules only when no other motion is pending.

Motion 14. To Rescind. The board may vote to rescind an action taken at a prior meeting, provided rescission is not forbidden by law.

> **Comment:** Each meeting of the board is in many respects a separate legal event. Consequently, and as noted in the *Comment* to Motion 13, the board may at a subsequent meeting undo an action taken at a previous meeting, except when prohibited by law, as when rescission would violate vested rights or result in the breach of a valid contract.
>
> In contrast to a motion to reconsider, a motion to rescind may be made at any time, and by any member, after the meeting at which the action to be reversed was taken.

Motion 15. To Prevent Reintroduction for [Six] Months. This motion may be used to prevent the reintroduction of a failed substantive motion for a time, but it is in order only when made immediately following the substantive motion's defeat. To be

---

106. In its section on motions to reconsider, *Robert's* acknowledges that, when a motion requires a supermajority for adoption, the minority can be the "prevailing side" if the motion fails. *Id.* at 315, ll. 34–36; 316, l. 1.

adopted, this motion must receive affirmative votes equal to at least two-thirds of the board's total membership, excluding vacant seats. If this motion is adopted, the ban on reintroduction remains in effect for [six] months or until the board's next organizational meeting, whichever occurs first.

> **Comment:** This "clincher" motion can be used to prevent a member from introducing the same motion again and again when the board as a whole has no desire to consider it further. The objection to consideration of a question in *Robert's* serves a similar purpose.[107]
>
> The elevated vote requirement for this motion recognizes that members should not lightly act to curtail another member's right to bring a matter before the board. If the board later wishes to take up the matter during the period in which reintroduction is forbidden, it may do so by suspending the rules under Motion 6.
>
> Six months is merely a suggested time; the board may shorten or lengthen the time as it sees fit. In order to give new board members a clean slate, the motion cannot be effective beyond the board's next organizational meeting.

Rule 26. Debate

The presiding officer shall state the motion and then open the floor to debate, presiding over the debate according to the principles listed below.

- The maker of the motion is entitled to speak first.
- A member who has not spoken on the issue shall be recognized before a member who has already spoken.
- To the extent practicable, debate shall alternate between proponents and opponents of the measure.

---

107. *Id.* at 267, ll. 16–20 ("The purpose of an *Objection to the Consideration of a Question* is to enable the assembly to avoid a particular original main motion altogether when it believes it would be strongly undesirable for the motion even to come before the assembly.").

- [No member may speak more than twice on the same substantive motion. A member's first speech on a substantive motion shall be limited to [ten] minutes, and any second speech on the same motion shall be limited to [five] minutes. The same rules apply to debate on a procedural motion, except that a member's first speech shall not exceed [five] minutes, and any second speech shall be limited to [two] minutes.]

    Comment: The first three principles set out in this rule follow guidelines for debate found in *Robert's Rules of Order.*[108] The suggested provision in brackets at the end of this rule is similar to Rule 10(b) in the procedural rules for the North Carolina House of Representatives. Not all local government boards will want to include the suggested language, and any board that decides to adopt it should carefully evaluate whether its proposed time limits suit the board's particular situation.

Rule 27. Adoption by Majority Vote

A motion is adopted if supported by a simple majority of the votes cast, a quorum being present, except when a larger majority is required by these rules or state law.

> **Comment:** Consistent with standard parliamentary practice, Rule 27 provides that a motion generally passes if supported by more than half of the votes cast, so long as a quorum is present.[109] State law articulates different majority requirements for certain local government appointed boards. For a water and sewer authority to take action, for example, a motion must be supported by a majority of the authority's total membership, not just a majority of a quorum.[110] Likewise, the concurring

---

108. *Id.* at 379, ll. 10–13, ll. 27–35; 380, ll. 1–2.

109. "[T]he basic requirement for approval of an action or choice by a deliberative assembly, except where a rule provides otherwise, is a *majority vote.* The word *majority* means 'more than half'; and when the term *majority vote* is used without qualification . . . it means more than half of the votes cast by persons entitled to vote, excluding blanks or abstentions, at a regular or properly called meeting." *Id.* at 400, ll. 5–12 (emphases in original).

110. G.S. 162A-5(c).

votes of four-fifths of a board of adjustment are needed to grant a variance.[111] Several of the procedural motions listed in Rule 25 also require more than a simple majority for adoption. Board members should consult the local government attorney if they are unclear about the number of affirmative votes necessary to adopt a particular motion.

Rule 28. Changing a Vote

A member may change the member's vote on a motion at any time before the presiding officer announces whether the motion has passed or failed. Once the presiding officer announces the result, a member may not change a vote without the unanimous consent of the remaining members present. A member's request for unanimous consent to change a vote is not in order unless made immediately following the presiding officer's announcement of the result.

---

111. G.S. 160D-406(i). *See also id.* §§ 63-81(c) ("No action, other than an action to recess or adjourn, shall be taken except upon a majority vote of the entire authorized membership of [a special airport] district board."); 159B-9(e) (For a joint municipal electric power agency, "[a] majority of the votes which the commissioners present are entitled to cast shall be necessary and sufficient to take any action or to pass any resolution, provided that such commissioners present are entitled to cast a majority of the votes of all commissioners of the board."); 159B-11(b) ("No joint [municipal power electric power] agency shall undertake any project required to be financed, in whole or in part, with the proceeds of bonds without the approval of a majority of its members."); 159B-43(e) ("Except as specifically provided by the bylaws, a majority of the votes of the [joint municipal assistance agency] commissioners present shall be necessary and sufficient to take any action or to pass any resolution."); 159C-4(d) ("The affirmative vote of a majority of the commissioners of [a county industrial facilities and pollution control financing] authority then in office shall be necessary for any action taken by the authority."); 160A-577 ("[A]n affirmative vote of the majority of the members present at a meeting of [a public transportation] authority shall be required to constitute action of the authority."); 162A-34(a) ("[T]he affirmative vote of a majority of the members of the [metropolitan water] district board present at any meeting thereof shall be necessary for any action taken by the district board."); 162A-67(d) (same for metropolitan sewerage district board); 162A-85.3(f) (same for metropolitan water and sewerage district); 163-33(2) ("In exercising the powers and duties of this subdivision, the [county board of elections] may act only when a majority of its members are present at any meeting at which such powers or duties are exercised.").

Comment: This rule largely adopts but also simplifies the approach taken by *Robert's Rules of Order* to vote changes.[112] The steps for obtaining unanimous consent are described in the *Comment* to Rule 20.

Rule 29. Duty to Vote

[Members may abstain from voting by so indicating when the vote is taken.] [Every member shall vote unless excused by the remaining members of the board. A member who wishes to be excused from voting shall so inform the presiding officer, who shall take a vote of the remaining members on whether to grant the request. The board may not excuse a member except in cases involving (1) a conflict of interest as defined by law or the board or (2) the member's official conduct or own financial interest.] [The unexcused failure to vote by a member who is physically present in the meeting room, or who has withdrawn without being excused by majority vote of the remaining members present, shall be recorded as [an affirmative vote] [a negative vote]].

> **Comment:** Some local appointed boards allow their members to abstain from voting, but others do not. Either approach is legally acceptable.[113] Boards that wish to allow abstentions should adopt the first bracketed sentence in Rule 29 and omit the other language. Boards that disfavor abstentions should delete the first bracketed sentence and adopt the second bracketed sentence, which imposes on members a duty to vote except in situations involving (1) conflicts of interest, as defined by state law or the board or (2) the members' official conduct or financial interests. State law, for instance, forbids a planning board member from voting on a proposed zoning ordinance amendment or zoning map amendment "where the

---

112. See *RONR* (11th ed.), p. 408, ll. 21–36; 409, ll. 1–10 (detailing the steps necessary for a vote change).

113. Such flexibility is not available to city council members and county commissioners, all of whom have a statutory duty to vote unless excused for valid reasons. G.S. 153A-44 (describing grounds on which county commissioners may be excused from voting); 160A-75 (same for city council members).

outcome of the matter being considered is reasonably likely to have a direct, substantial, and readily identifiable financial impact on the member."[114]

If a board imposes a duty to vote on its members, it may also want to adopt the final sentence in Rule 29, which sets out the consequence of a member's unexcused failure to vote: The member is recorded as having voted anyway. A board that adopts the final sentence must decide whether such a member will be recorded as having voted in the affirmative or in the negative. The inspiration for the final sentence comes from G.S. 160A-75, which mandates that a city council member's unexcused failure to vote be recorded as an affirmative vote, except when the vote concerns zoning ordinances or rezonings.

Rule 30. Voting by Written Ballot

(a) **Secret Ballots Prohibited.** The board shall not vote by secret ballot.

(b) **Rules for Written Ballots.** The board may decide by majority vote or unanimous consent to vote on a motion by written ballot. Each member shall sign his or her ballot, and the minutes shall record how each member voted by name. The ballots shall be made available for public inspection in the office of the [clerk][secretary] to the board immediately following the meeting at which the vote took place and remain there until the minutes of that meeting are approved, at which time the ballots may be destroyed.

> **Comment:** Rule 30 paraphrases the open meetings law's provisions on a public body's use of written ballots.[115] Although the board may decide by majority vote to cast written ballots on a motion, Rule 30(b) also allows it to make such a determination

---

114. G.S. 160D-109(b). *See also id.* § 157-5(b) ("No commissioner who is also a person directly assisted by the public housing authority shall be qualified to vote on matters affecting his or her official conduct or matters affecting his or her own individual tenancy, as distinguished from matters affecting tenants in general.").
115. G.S. 143-318.13(b).

by unanimous consent to avoid the awkwardness of members voting on how to vote. The steps for obtaining unanimous consent are described in the *Comment* to Rule 20.

Part IX. Public Hearings
Rule 31. Public Hearings
(a) Calling Public Hearings. The board may hold public hearings to solicit the public's input on specific issues. The board may schedule its public hearings or delegate that responsibility to staff members, as appropriate.

> **Comment:** Some local government boards have to hold public hearings. In more than one jurisdiction, for example, the zoning ordinance directs the planning board to conduct public hearings on proposed changes to the zoning map. Other appointed boards may find it useful to hold public hearings even when they are not required to do so. Rule 31(a) affords them that flexibility.

(b) Public Hearing Locations. The board may hold public hearings anywhere within the area served by the board.

> **Comment:** Rule 31(b) echoes the geographic restrictions imposed by state law on public hearings held by city councils and boards of county commissioners.[116]

(c) Notice of Public Hearings. Any public hearing attended by a majority of members shall be considered part of a regular or special meeting of the board. Consequently, the relevant notice and related requirements of the open meetings law, as set out in Rules 9 through 12, apply to such hearings. If a hearing's subject matter triggers additional notice requirements under state law or local rules, the board shall see that they are also satisfied.

---

116. G.S. 153A-52 ("The board of [county] commissioners may hold public hearings at any place within the county."); 160A-81 ("Public hearings may be held at any place within the city or within the county in which the city is located.").

Comment: A public hearing triggers the notice, minutes, and other requirements of the open meetings law if a majority of board members attend the hearing, as under those circumstances the event qualifies as an official meeting of the board.[117] Depending on the topic, the hearing may be subject to further notice requirements.

(d) Rules for Public Hearings. The board may adopt reasonable rules for public hearings that, among other things,

- fix the maximum time allotted to each speaker;
- provide for the designation of spokespersons for groups supporting or opposing the same positions;
- provide for the selection of delegates from groups supporting or opposing the same positions when the number of persons wishing to attend the hearing exceeds the capacity of the meeting room (so long as arrangements are made, in the case of a hearing subject to the open meetings law, for those excluded from the meeting room to listen to the hearing); and
- provide for the maintenance of order and decorum in the conduct of the hearing.

Comment: Rule 31(d) largely tracks statutory provisions that authorize city councils and boards of county commissioners to adopt reasonable rules for their public hearings.[118] In keeping with the spirit of the open meetings law, it also mandates that group members desiring to be present at a hearing covered by that law be given the opportunity to listen to the proceedings—outside the meeting room if necessary—if the room is too small to accommodate them.

---

117. G.S. 143-318.10(d) (emphasis added) (official meeting of public body occurs when majority of its members gather in person or simultaneously by electronic means "for the purpose of *conducting hearings,* participating in deliberations, or voting upon or otherwise transacting the public business within the jurisdiction, real or apparent, of the public body").

118. G.S. 153A-52 (conduct of public hearings by board of county commissioners), 160A-81 (conduct of public hearings by city council).

(e) Continuing Public Hearings. The board may continue any public hearing without further advertisement, provided the time (including the date, if the hearing will resume on a different day) and place of the continued hearing are announced in open session. Except for hearings conducted pursuant to paragraph (g) of this rule, if a quorum of the board is not present for a properly scheduled public hearing, the hearing shall be continued until the board's next regular meeting without further advertisement.

> **Comment:** Rule 31(e) borrows from the legal rules for continuing a public hearing called by a city council or board of county commissioners.[119]

(f) Conduct of Public Hearings. At the time appointed for the hearing, the chair shall call the hearing to order and proceed to allow public input in accordance with any rules adopted by the board for the hearing. Unless the board votes to extend the hearing, when the time allotted for the hearing expires, or when no one wishes to speak who has not already done so, the chair shall declare the hearing closed, and the board shall resume the regular order of business.

(g) Public Hearings by Less Than a Majority of Board Members. Unless inconsistent with state law or local rules, the board may appoint a member or members to hold a public hearing on its behalf. The notice provisions in paragraph (c) of this rule apply when the board appoints more than one member to conduct such a hearing.

> **Comment:** A board may appoint one or more members short of a quorum to conduct a public hearing that is not required by law. When the board authorizes more than one member to conduct a public hearing, the safe course of action with regard to the open meetings law is to assume that the members tasked with holding the hearing constitute a committee of the board and that the hearing is therefore subject to the law's public notice and related requirements for special meetings.

---

119. G.S. 153A-52 (continuation of public hearing by board of county commissioners); 160A-81 (continuation of public hearing by city council).

(h) Public Comment. The board may hold a public comment period at any regular meeting or special meeting called, at least in part, for that purpose. During the public comment period, members of the public may speak on any matters within the board's real or apparent jurisdiction. The provisions in paragraphs (d) and (f) of this rule apply to the board's public comment periods.

> **Comment:** State law requires city councils, boards of county commissioners, and local boards of education to hold public comment periods periodically.[120] Although no statutes direct any local government appointed boards to do the same, some appointed boards may find the practice beneficial. The board has the same authority to adopt procedural rules for public comment periods that it enjoys with respect to public hearings. As with public hearings, the presiding officer should formally open and close the public comment period.

Part X. Committees and Appointments
Rule 32. Committees
(a) Authority to Establish. [The board][The chair] may establish standing or temporary committees to help the board carry out its work. Rule 33(b) governs appointments to all such committees.

> **Comment:** Many local government boards have committees that aid them in their work. In general, board action is necessary to create a committee unless the board has delegated that power to the chair.[121] The chair of a local economic development commission has statutory authority to establish any committees necessary to assist the commission.[122]

---

120. G.S. 115C-51 (public comment period for local board of education); 153A-52.1 (same for board of county commissioners); 160A-81.1 (same for city council).

121. *See* G.S. 160D-303(a) (historic preservation commission "may appoint advisory bodies and committees as appropriate").

122. G.S. 158-9.

(b) Open Meetings Law. The requirements of the open meetings law apply whenever a majority of a committee's members gather in person or simultaneously by electronic means to discuss or otherwise conduct committee business.

> **Comment:** Rule 32(b) tracks the open meetings law's definition of "official meeting."[123] Official meetings of local government bodies trigger the notice, access, and related requirements of the open meetings law, regardless of whether the body is labeled a committee, board, commission, or some other term.[124]

Rule 33. Appointments to Public Bodies

(a) Appointments in Open Session. To the extent that it appoints its own members or the members of other public bodies, the board shall consider and make appointments in open session.

> **Comment:** The open meetings law expressly prohibits a public body from meeting in closed session to consider or make appointments to other public bodies. It also forbids a public body from meeting in closed session to consider or fill a vacancy among its own membership.[125]
>
> The default rule is that the authority to name members to a local appointed board lies with the governing body that created the board, usually a city council or board of county commissioners.[126] The governing body may delegate this appointment authority to the board, except where state law mandates that the governing body make

---

123. G.S. 143-318.10(d).

124. *See* G.S. 143-318.10(b) (emphasis added) (defining a "public body" for purposes of the open meetings law to include, *inter alia*, "any elected or appointed authority, board, commission, *committee,* council, or other body of . . . one or more counties, cities, [or] school administrative units, . . . that (i) is composed of two or more members and (ii) exercises or is authorized to exercise a legislative, policy-making, quasi-judicial, administrative, or advisory function").

125. G.S. 143-318.11(a)(6).

126. *See* G.S. 160D-310 ("Unless specified otherwise by statute or local ordinance, all appointments to boards authorized by [G.S. Chapter 160D] shall be made by the governing board of the local government.").

the appointments.[127] In a few cases, state law authorizes appointed boards to select one or more of their members.[128]

---

127. G.S. 18B-700(b), (c) (city or county governing body to appoint local ABC board); 122C-118.1(a) (board(s) of county commissioners to appoint area authority board); 130A-35(b) (board of county commissioners to appoint county board of health); 130A-45.1(b) ("In a single county authority, the county board of commissioners shall appoint the members of the [public health authority] board[.]"); 139-41(b) (board of county commissioners to appoint watershed improvement commission); 153A-77(c) (board of county commissioners to appoint consolidated human services board from nominees presented by that board); 153A-423(a) (regional solid waste management authority board to be "composed of delegates to the authority who shall be appointed by and serve at the pleasure of the governing boards of their respective units of local government"); 158-21 (board of county commissioners to appoint industrial development commission); 160A-553 (city council to appoint parking authority); 160A-577 (governing body to appoint public transportation authority); 160D-302(a) (governing body to appoint board of adjustment); 160D-304(a) (same for appearance commission); 162A-5 (members of water and sewer authority "to be selected by the respective political subdivision"); 162A-34 (appointments to metropolitan water district board made by board of county commissioners and political subdivisions included in the district); 162A-85.3(a) (appointment authority for metropolitan water and sewerage district board).

The statutes for some appointed boards do not require the governing body to appoint members, but they do direct the governing body to establish procedures for filling vacancies on those boards. G.S. 105-322 (board of equalization and review); 153A-265 (library board of trustees); 153A-392(2) (regional planning commission); 160A-472(3) (regional council of government); 160A-479.4(3) (regional sports authority).

128. For a three-member county board of social services, the board of county commissioners picks one member, the state's Social Services Commission picks the second member, and those two members select the third. G.S. 108A-3(a). For a five-member board, the board of county commissioners and the Social Services Commission select two members each, and those four members designate the fifth member. Id. § 108A-3(b). See also id. §§ 108A-15.8(c) (members of regional social services board to fill any remaining vacancies on the board after pertinent boards of county commissioners and Social Services Commission have made their appointments); 130A-37(b) (board of county commissioners of each county in district appoints one commissioner to district board of health (BOH); district BOH members appoint other members); 130A-45.1(b) ("[I]n [a public health] authority comprising two or more counties, the chair of the county board of commissioners of each county in the authority shall appoint one county commissioner, or the commissioner's express designee, to the authority board and these members shall jointly appoint the other members of the board.").

In others, the law vests appointment authority in the mayor or the chair of the board of county commissioners.[129] Both the State Board of Elections and the Governor play a role in appointing county boards of elections.[130]

(b) Committee Appointments. [The board][The chair] shall make appointments to any committees established under Rule 32. When a committee is to include non-board members selected by the board, the board will appoint such persons in open session using the procedures described below.

> **Comment:** The board's committees may be composed of board members only, of other persons only, or of a combination of board members and other persons. Rule 33(b) invites the board to decide whether it will make committee appointments or delegate that power to the chair. The chair of a local economic-development commission has express statutory authority to "appoint such committees as the work of the commission may require."[131] The chair of a regional planning commission "may appoint any committees authorized by the [commission's] bylaws."[132]

---

129. G.S. 131E-18(d) (mayor or chair of board of county commissioners to appoint replacement members of hospital authority board from list of nominees submitted by board); 143B-1254 (mayor to appoint initial members of veterans' recreation authority but vacancies to be filled by mayor and remaining commissioners acting unanimously); 157-5 (mayor to appoint housing authority members); 130A-45.1(b) ("[I]n [a public health authority comprising two or more counties, the chair of the county board of commissioners of each county in the authority shall appoint one county commissioner, or the commissioner's express designee, to the authority board and these members shall jointly appoint the other members of the board.").

130. G.S. 163-30(a) (State Board of Elections to appoint four members of county board of elections, with Governor appointing fifth member, who serves as chair). *See also* G.S. 160A-684(b) (Governor appoints one member, General Assembly appoints two members, and Secretary of Department of Transportation appoints three members of ferry transportation authority board.). The clerk of court appoints drainage district commissioners. *Id.* § 156-81(a).

131. G.S. 158-9.

132. G.S. 153A-394.

(c) Appointment by Unanimous Consent. When there is only one nominee, the chair may ask the board to approve the nominee's appointment by unanimous consent. If any member objects, the board shall vote on the nomination in accordance with paragraph (d) or (e) of this rule, whichever applies.

> **Comment:** Formal voting procedures may not be needed when there is only one nominee for a position. Rule 33(c) allows the board to make an appointment in that situation through the unanimous consent procedure described in the *Comment* to Rule 20.

(d) Nomination and Voting Procedure. The board shall use the following procedure in making appointments. [The nominating committee shall be called upon to make its report and recommendation(s), if any.] The chair shall [then] open the floor for nominations, whereupon board members may put forward and debate nominees. When debate ends, the chair shall call the roll of the members, and each member shall cast a vote for the member's preferred nominee. Voting shall continue until a nominee receives a majority of votes cast during a single balloting.

> **Comment:** Rule 33(d) recommends that the board make appointments through a nomination procedure. An alternative way of proceeding is by motion. A member moves that the board appoint an individual, and following debate, the board votes on the motion. If the motion passes, the seat is filled. If it fails, the floor is then open to a new motion. One downside to the appointment-by-motion method is that it puts members who prefer other candidates in the uncomfortable position of having to vote against the person named in the motion. The nomination procedure allows each member to vote for a preferred candidate without having to vote against anyone else.
>
> As implied by the optional language in brackets, some local government boards may wish to use nominating committees to consider and recommend appointments.

(e) Multiple Appointments. If the board is making more than one appointment to a body, each member shall have as many votes in each balloting as there are slots to be filled, and the votes of a majority of the total number of members voting shall be required for each appointment. No member may cast more than one vote for the same candidate for the same position during a single balloting.

> **Comment:** Rule 33(e) explains how the procedure set out in Rule 33(d) works when more than one appointment is being made to the same body.

(f) Vote by Written Ballot. The board may vote on proposed appointments by written ballot in accordance with Rule 30.

> **Comment:** Written ballots may also be used if the board employs the appointment-by-motion method. Rules for public access under Rule 30(b) apply.

Part XI. Miscellaneous
Rule 34. Amendment of the Rules

The board may vote to amend these rules at any regular meeting or at any properly called special meeting for which amendment of the rules is one of the meeting's stated purposes. Any amendment to these rules must not violate any relevant statutes or generally accepted principles of parliamentary procedure. To be adopted, a motion to amend these rules must be approved by a majority of the board's members [and submitted to the [city council] [board of county commissioners] for approval].

> **Comment:** As remarked in the *Comment* to Rule 1, local government appointed boards may adopt procedural rules that do not conflict with state law or generally accepted parliamentary principles. That same authority extends to the amendment of such rules. In some places, however, appointed boards operate under rules adopted for them by their respective city councils or boards of county commissioners. Those appointed boards may need to submit proposed rule changes to their governing bodies, a possibility contemplated by the bracketed language in Rule 34.

A majority of a board's members, rather than a simple majority of votes cast, is necessary to approve proposed amendments to these rules. Without this requirement, a minority of the members might be tempted to alter these rules when other members are absent to allow for some action disfavored by most of their colleagues.

Rule 34 should not be confused with a motion to suspend the rules under Rule 25 (Motion 6).

Rule 35. Reference to *Robert's Rules of Order Newly Revised*

The board shall refer to *Robert's Rules of Order Newly Revised* for guidance when confronted with a procedural issue not covered by these rules or state law. Having consulted *Robert's*, the presiding officer shall make a ruling on the issue subject to appeal to the board under Rule 25 (Motion 1).

> **Comment:** Because *Robert's* was written chiefly with large assemblies in mind, many of its provisions may not be ideal for a small board. Except insofar as they embody general principles of parliamentary procedure, the provisions in *Robert's* should be viewed as purely advisory in nature. They do not bind the board.

Rule 36. Special Rules of Procedure

The board may adopt its own special rules of procedure, to be specified here.

> **Comment:** Some boards may wish to provide special rules for situations not contemplated by these suggested rules. If a board sees no need for any special rules, it should omit Rule 36 from its adoption of these suggested rules.

Appendix A. Procedural Statutes for Some Local Appointed Boards in North Carolina

Topic	N.C. General Statute(s)
Alcoholic Beverage Control	
Alcoholic Beverage Control Board	G.S. 18B-700
Animal Control	
Dangerous Dog Board (Initial Determinations)	G.S. 67-4.1
Dangerous Dog Board (Appeals)	G.S. 67-4.1
Economic Development	
County Industrial Facilities and Pollution Control Financing Authority	G.S. 159C-4, -6 to -8, -10, -16
Economic Development Commission	G.S. 158-8 to -9
Facility Authority	G.S. 160A-480.3
Industrial Development Commission	G.S. 158-21
Joint Redevelopment Commission	G.S. 160A-507.1
Redevelopment Commission (City)	G.S. 160A-504
Redevelopment Commission (County)	G.S. 160A-506
Regional Sports Authority	G.S. 160A-479.4 to -479.5
Regional Planning and Development Commission	G.S. 158-14
Regional Planning and Economic Development Commission	G.S. 153A-398
Regional Planning Commission	G.S. 153A-392 to -394
Regional Redevelopment Commission	G.S. 160A-507
Elections	
Board of Elections	G.S. 163-30 to -33.1
Electric Power	
Joint Municipal Electric Power Agency	G.S. 159B-9 to -11
Joint Municipal Assistance Agency	G.S. 159B-43 to -43.1
Fire	
Fire Protection District Commission	G.S. 69-25.7

Health

Area Mental Health, Developmental Disabilities, and Substance Abuse Authority Board	G.S. 122C-116, -118.1 to -120
Board of Health (County)	G.S. 130A-24, -35, -39
Board of Health (District)	G.S. 130A-24, -37, -39
Board of Health (Public Health Authority Board)	G.S. 130A-45.1
Consolidated Human Services Board	G.S. 130A-24, -39, -43; 153A-77
County Commissioner Advisory Board to Area Mental Health, Developmental Disabilities, and Substance Abuse Authority	G.S. 122C-118.2
Mosquito Control District	G.S. 130A-354

Hospitals

Municipal Hospital Governing Authority	G.S. 131E-9
Hospital Authority Board of Commissioners	G.S. 131E-18, -21 to -22

Housing

Housing Authority (City)	G.S. 157-5 to -8
Housing Authority (County)	G.S. 157-34
Housing Authority (Regional)	G.S. 157-36
Housing Authority (Consolidated)	G.S. 157-39.5

Land Use[a]

Appearance Commission	G.S. 160D-304
Board of Adjustment	G.S. 160D-302, -406
Historic Preservation Commission	G.S. 160D-303
Housing Appeals Board	G.S. 160D-305
Planning Board	G.S. 160D-301, -604
Regional Planning Commission	G.S. 153A-392, -394

Libraries

Library Board of Trustees	G.S. 153A-265 to -266

---

a. All the boards listed in this section are potentially subject to G.S. 160D-307 (extraterritorial representation on boards).

Natural Resources and Environment

County Industrial Facilities and Pollution Control Financing Authority	G.S. 159C-4
Drainage District	G.S. 156-79, -81
Metropolitan Sewerage District	G.S. 162A-67
Metropolitan Water and Sewerage District	G.S. 162A-85.3
Metropolitan Water District	G.S. 162A-34
Regional Natural Gas District	G.S. 160A-664 to -665, -671, -676
Regional Solid Waste Management Authority	G.S. 153A-423 to -425
Multi-County Water Conservation and Infrastructure District	G.S. 158-15.1
Water and Sewer Authority	G.S. 162A-5
Watershed Improvement Commission	G.S. 139-41

Parks and Recreation

Parks and Recreation Commission	G.S. 160A-354
Veterans' Recreation Authority	G.S. 143B-1253, -1254, -1258

Regional Council of Governments

Regional Council of Government	G.S. 160A-472, -473

Social Services

Social Services Board (County)	G.S. 108A-1 to -7
Social Services Board (Regional)	G.S. 108A-15.8
Consolidated Human Services Board	G.S. 108A-15.1; 153A-77

Taxation

Board of Equalization and Review	G.S. 105-322
Special Tax Board for Regional Public Transportation Authority	G.S. 160A-607.1

Transportation

Ferry Transportation Authority	G.S. 160A-683 to -684
Parking Authority	G.S. 160A-553
Public Transportation Authority	G.S. 160A-577
Regional Public Transportation Authority	G.S. 160A-605 to -606
Regional Transportation Authority	G.S. 160A-633, -635 to -636
Special Airport District	G.S. 63-81

Appendix B. Order of Precedence for Procedural Motions

The chart below summarizes the procedural motions permitted under Rule 25. All are debatable, and none requires a second. All may be amended, subject to the stated limitations on motions to amend (Rule 25, Motion 11).

Most procedural motion pass if supported by a simple majority—more than half—of votes cast, a quorum being present. For reasons explained in the *Comments* to Rule 25, a supermajority is necessary to adopt a motion to suspend the rules (Motion 6) or a motion to prevent reintroduction (Motion 15).

Motion	Vote Required	Notes
1. To Appeal a Ruling of the Presiding Officer	Majority	This motion is in order immediately after the ruling being appealed and at no other time. The member making the motion need not be recognized, and, if timely, the motion may not be ruled out of order.
2. To Adjourn	Majority	This motion is not in order if the board is in closed session.
3. To Recess to a Time and Place Certain	Majority	The motion must state the time (including the date if the meeting will reconvene on a different day) and place at which the meeting will resume. It is not in order if the board is in closed session.
4. To Take a Brief Recess	Majority	None.
5. To Follow the Agenda	Majority	This motion must be made when an item of business that deviates from the agenda is proposed or it is out of order as to that item.

Motion	Vote Required	Notes
6. To Suspend the Rules	Two-thirds of entire membership, excluding vacant seats	The board may not suspend provisions that incorporate state law.
7. To Defer Consideration	Majority	A substantive motion that is deferred expires [100] days after the deferral date unless a timely motion to revive consideration (Motion 13) is adopted. While a deferred motion remains pending, a new motion with the same effect may not be introduced unless the board first votes to suspend its rules (Motion 6).
8. To End Debate (Call the Previous Question)	Majority	Any substantive or procedural motion is potentially subject to a motion to end debate. A motion to end debate on a pending motion is not in order until every member has had a chance to speak once.
9. To Postpone to a Certain Time	Majority	This motion may be used to delay consideration of a substantive motion until a designated day, meeting, or hour. While a postponed motion remains pending, a new motion with the same effect may not be introduced unless the board first votes to suspend its rules (Motion 6).
10. To Refer a Motion to a Committee	Majority	If the committee fails to report on the motion within [60] days, the board must take up the referred motion again at the request of the member who introduced it. During the referral period, a substantive motion with the same effect may not be introduced unless the board first votes to suspend its rules (Motion 6).
11. To Amend	Majority	Any substantive or any procedural motion other than a motion to appeal (Motion 1) may be amended. A motion to amend must concern the same subject matter as the motion that it seeks to alter. No more than one motion to amend and one motion to amend the amendment may be pending at the same time.
12. To Revive Consideration	Majority	This motion is in order within [100] days of the vote to defer consideration (Motion 7).

Motion	Vote Required	Notes
13. To Reconsider	Majority	To be in order, this motion must be made by a member of the prevailing side at the same meeting during which the original vote was taken. The motion may not interrupt deliberation on a pending matter.
14. To Rescind	Majority	This motion is not in order if rescission is forbidden by law.
15. To Prevent Reintroduction For [Six] Months	Two-thirds of entire membership, excluding vacant seats	This motion is in order immediately following the defeat of a substantive motion and at no other time. If adopted, it bars the reintroduction of the failed substantive motion for [six] months or until the board's next organizational meeting, whichever comes first. If the board wishes to take up the substantive motion during the period in which reintroduction is forbidden, it must first vote to suspend its rules (Motion 6).

www.ingramcontent.com/pod-product-compliance
Lightning Source LLC
Chambersburg PA
CBHW061838220326
41599CB00027B/5327